Continued from front flap

aware of it—and even unconsciously affected by it.

Our practical need, if we are to have a viable future, is to replace that Manichaean hostility to Nature with a kind of 'cosmic piety', a recognition that the world is a good and lovely thing, to be cherished even at some cost in material comfort and economic expansion.

"A recovered cosmic piety might enable us to sit still and get our breath back and remember what peace and quiet were like, discovering also the human value of neighbourhood living and a neighbourhood economy."

He asks, "Do we really want to live in urban apartments or suburban houses, working all day at the factory or the office, and then coming home to processed food and mechanised entertainment?

"All the evidence suggests that apart from the single question of medicine we would be much happier in a much simpler kind of society, technological up to a point, but cautiously resolute in the subordination of technical means to real human ends." And finally:

"If the environmental crisis kills us all, as some well-informed people fear it may, we shall die by our own collective hand, rejecting life. But it may not be so serious, it is probably not too late, and there are signs that the tide is turning here and there. We have time, in all probability, to learn the lesson and thus preach and practice a little 'cosmic piety': and we have certainly both time and cause for gratitude.

"It would be good manners, on our part, to make this a daily habit—to make it the whole of our prayers, if it comes to that, but at least their starting-point. And then, on some windy morning, we might open our eyes and for the first time catch sight of this world, our rare and fragile home."

The Delicate Creation

Books by Christopher Derrick

The Moral and Social Teaching of the Church
LONDON: BURNS, OATES   NEW YORK: HAWTHORN BOOKS

Trimming the Ark:
Catholic Attitudes and the Cult of Change
NEW YORK: P. J. KENEDY   LONDON: HUTCHINSON   PARIS: FAYARD

Reader's Report
on the Writing of Novels
LONDON: GOLLANCZ   BOSTON: THE WRITER, INC.

Honest Love and Human Life:
Is the Pope Right about Contraception?
LONDON: HUTCHINSON   NEW YORK: COWARD-MC CANN

The Delicate Creation:
Towards a Theology of the Environment
OLD GREENWICH: DEVIN-ADAIR   LONDON: TOM STACEY

The

Delicate Creation

Towards a Theology of

the Environment

BY

Christopher Derrick

FOREWORD

BY

René Dubos, M.D.

INTRODUCTION

BY

John Cardinal Wright

❋

The Devin-Adair Company

Old Greenwich

Conn.

Foreword

❈

Modern society is torn between two contrasting attitudes concerning the environmental crisis. Some of us respond to it by advocating "complete technological domination" over Nature. Others "drop out and tune in ecstatically to some private wave length" of existence. As Christopher Derrick points out, however, we shall not get anywhere by thinking in such negative terms about the environment, and by concentrating upon the "evils of technomania." What is needed is "a revived sense of the goodness and holiness" of creation. I agree with Christopher Derrick that this sense is implied in orthodox Christian teachings. But I have more confidence than he seems to have in the possibility of recapturing it through scientific knowledge of man's place in the cosmos.

I found myself much more in resonance with Christopher Derrick's book than I had expected. I suspect in fact that his attitude and mine are fundamentally the same—only two different expressions of the same intellectual faith.

RENÉ DUBOS

Rockefeller University, N.Y.

Introduction

❋

Christopher Derrick is something of a maverick: he cannot be fitted at all easily into the pattern of our current partisanships—of conservative and liberal, of traditionalist and progressive. If we have to dichotomise on such lines as these, we shall usually find him partly on both sides and partly on neither side. He walks the middle road, but in the spirit of Chesterton's *Orthodoxy*, seeking no mere neutrality or compromise but rather the balanced tension of opposites. And like anybody else who walks a middle road, he is liable to be attacked—or, even worse, to be ignored—by the extremists on either side.

I introduce this book gladly, in the belief that he and his work ought to be more widely known. What struck me most forcibly, on first reading *The Delicate Creation*, was the subtlety with which he establishes a middle position—a balanced position, doing full justice to both extremes—in connection with the visible universe, the world of our daily experience. He is discussing our treatment of this world, our attitude towards it, in the context of what we now call 'the environmental crisis'; and he makes it very clear that this is a field in which two equal and opposite mistakes are possible. On the one hand we can make the mistake of the materialist: we can suppose that this world, and the observable universe beyond it, constitutes the whole of reality and is therefore the only thing that we need to worry about. In general, religious people at least are aware of this mistake and on their guard against it. But they may be less keenly on their guard against the converse mistake—the idea (often cherished by deeply spiritual people) that the material universe is somehow a contemptible thing, unimportant at the best, positively evil at the worst.

Derrick has the instincts of an artist, and is plainly far too deeply in love with this world to fall into that second mistake. But he is aware of it; and he reminds us in this book that it forms the basis of one of the most ancient, plausible, and persistent of the heresies—the heresy of the Manichees. His point —and it seems to me a most interesting and important point— is that this ancient heresy is far from dead. Variously disguised, it flourishes in our time, and lies at the heart of many apparently new tendencies in thought, in literature and the arts, and even in religion. Against Manichaeanism, no less than against materialism, the wise man needs to be on his guard: the material universe is not the only thing that we need to be concerned with, nor the most important, but it is not to be regarded or treated with contempt.

Things of this kind have been said before: Derrick's originality lies in their application to the environmental crisis. We are stuck with this crisis because—for many years now—we have seen our destiny in terms of 'Man's Conquest of Nature': that is, we have seen the visible world as an enemy, a thing to be beaten down and then exploited. Experts in various fields are now drawing our attention to the very serious dangers so created: Derrick suggests, very plausibly, that we have acted in this suicidal way because our society cherishes—at some level in its collective unconscious—a basically hostile or Manichaean attitude towards the world, the environment. And so, if we are to surmount the present crisis, new methods and new techniques will not be enough. We shall need to go deeper: as Derrick puts it, we shall need to repent of a heresy.

Even so, this is not simply a 'religious' book: it should interest not only those with a concern for doctrinal truth, but also those who do not care to look beyond the boundaries of their physical environment. To such readers as those, Derrick addresses a somewhat impassioned plea: not merely for God's sake, but for the world's sake and their own sake as well, they should cultivate the habit of 'cosmic piety', of care and veneration for this delicate world of ours. Scripture tells us that God made it, looked upon it in its springtime, and found it good: even those who do not believe in the Scriptures or in God still need to respect the principle so expressed, and to control the world-despising and domineering instinct that is so rapidly converting the good world into a mess charged with menace.

I strongly suspect that this is an approach which will delight and also infuriate a great many people. Derrick shares the environmental and ecological anxieties which are so often expressed by the liberal intelligentsia, and will probably capture their goodwill initially; but they are not likely to relish his deeply theological interpretation, and I expect them to howl with anger at his firm refusal to adopt the fashionably Manichaean attitude towards population and birth-control. Conversely, many religious people who still keep "the faith once delivered to the saints" will recognise in Derrick an ally, a defender of orthodoxy against the modernisms and the half-Christianities; but they may regret the limited and particular purpose of this book. There is no attempt here to re-assert the whole body of Catholic faith, or to call people back to prayer and the sacraments, or to unite a divided Church: the emphasis is on one single though fundamental doctrine, the doctrine which we find on the first page of the Bible and in the first words of the Creed——the doctrine that the materialist and the Manichee are equally and disastrously mistaken.

And so Derrick calls us back to a renewed love of creation, a new regard for its goodness and fragility: a habit of cosmic piety therefore, a sense of cosmic morality, a cosmic joy that will be rooted in gratitude. The worldly problem and the religious problem are not really separable. We chose to put God out of our culture and then we sinned against His works: we chose the world as an alternative to Him, treated it with contempt, and then fouled it up most suicidally. Paradoxically, the two extremes meet in practice. The materialist cares only for this world: the Manichee despises this world. But they turn out to behave in the same way and to be the same man— or at least, to be allies and brothers against the old central voice that still cries out in warning: "Behold, I have set before you life and death, a blessing and a curse. Choose therefore life, that thou and thy seed may live!"

It is that voice which is echoed here, in the words of a most lucid and exact writer. I recommend him for several different reasons, but perhaps most of all because in an age obsessed by domination and death, he speaks up for life.

JOHN CARDINAL WRIGHT

Vatican City, Easter, 1972

The Delicate Creation

One

Despite the generous beauty of this world and the abundant happiness that it offers, we live in what has often been called an age of anxiety; and now, as the twentieth century enters upon its last decades, it seems that we have manufactured for ourselves, needlessly, an entirely new kind of worry.

The matter is serious. Quite suddenly but with alarming force, it has dawned upon us that we are doing a number of very rash things to the fragile environment upon which we all depend, and that unless we change our habits soon and thoroughly—in a way that will not be easy and perhaps not possible—we are likely to inflict upon ourselves a most complex and unpleasant series of disasters. It has started already. Like Frankenstein's monster, our technologies have got out of hand: like the Sorcerer's Apprentice, we find ourselves unable to control the unexpectedly menacing forces that we mobilised unthinkingly to serve our needs of the moment.

It would be comforting to suppose that the consequent anxieties were exaggerated or groundless. They are certainly new. Only a few years ago, if some prophet of doom had warned us that we were doing dangerous and possibly suicidal things to the world and to ourselves, most of us would have dismissed him as a crank, an alarmist—possibly as a reactionary, contemptibly hooked upon nostalgia for the supposed beatitude of a simpler past, wretchedly hostile towards the great achievement and the greater future of technological man.

Things have certainly changed. 'The environmental crisis' has become part of the headline-news of every day: technological man is losing his old self-confidence, his belief in the wonderful future that was going to be ushered in by 'Man's Conquest of Nature'. We appear to be heading for disaster: the future has become a frightening thing.

In a sense, it was always frightening. There was always death, there was always war, civilisation was always a precarious thing: even before our present-day environmental worries, even before that Bomb, humanity's long-term prospects were depressing to think about with any realism. But progressively, over these last few years, they have become alarming in new ways—almost in new dimensions. We have come to fear not merely disaster but self-inflicted disaster, inexorably developing from activities that we had previously considered beneficial. Things were bad enough when we only had war to fear. There was the bombing aircraft, and then the long-range missile, and then the nuclear weapon; and then—more disturbingly, in a way—there came the discovery that the mere testing of these weapons, even in peacetime, endangered us all very seriously. But all these things were connected with actual or possible war; and we had known for a long time that the great god Mars has ugly ways and needs to be kept under control. The turning-point, the last straw came when we realised that precisely comparable dangers were arising in the context

of our wholly peaceful, wholly beneficent-seeming activities.

Thus the environmental and ecological problem came
into vision. It has now attracted an enormous amount of attention and initiated a great volume of discussion: popular
magazines devote whole issues and special features to it[1],
countless books are written about it[2], and politicians are
obliged to go through the motions of taking it very seriously. It has become a vogue-subject.

The questions so arising are enormously complex, but
their broad outlines are simple, and familiar by now to
most people. The trouble arises from the explosive development and multiplication of our technological activities.
Together with the scientific advances that lie behind them,
these activities constitute what we commonly call 'Man's
Conquest of Nature'; and it now turns out that alongside
the great benefits thus achieved, they carry with them—
not in rare instances but typically—a whole series of
unexpected side-effects, appearing slowly and not very
conspicuously at first, but alarmingly dangerous in the
long run.

The danger is threefold. In the first place, we are pollut-
ing the land and the water and the air with waste materials
of many kinds, on a scale that makes it possible for us to
starve or poison ourselves out of existence in the fairly
near future. In the second place, we are wasting the limited resources of this planet at a phenomenal speed, and
seem to be heading therefore for a collapse of the technologically complex society upon which we have come to depend. And in the third place, the particular technologies of
medicine and sanitation and public health have led to
sharply lower death-rates, in infancy and later, and thus to
the notorious 'population explosion'.

These three dangers are well known, and it is no part of this book's purpose to impart further information about them. Every day, we read some bizarre and horrifying news-item which makes the overall picture clearer and more frightening; and from such items, one can easily compile an illustrative catalogue of thoroughly nightmarish facts. At the present time, for example, the air of New York City has such a character that the citizen takes into his lungs the equivalent in toxic materials of thirty-eight cigarettes a day: that is, apart from the actual cigarettes that he smokes[3]. In the fatty tissues of his body, the average American now carries nearly twice the proportion of DDT that is considered tolerable in meat: Americans, a wit has observed, are unfit for human consumption[4]. Cannibalism may be rare in that country, at least during this present phase of the population-and-food story, but many mothers desire to feed their own babies; and this is a rash procedure, since that same very dangerous chemical is present in their breast-milk, at levels twice to six times as high as is permitted to the dairy industry[5]. If you draw your drinking water from Lake Michigan, as millions do, it is likely to contain cyanide[6]; if you buy lettuces in Montana, they are likely to contain one hundred and twenty times the tolerable proportion of lead [7]. California's garbage, accumulated for one year, would build a wall a hundred feet wide and thirty feet high, stretching right down that state, all the way from Oregon to Mexico[8]. The Rhine is so heavily polluted that even eels, which are hardy fish, find it difficult to survive in that 'sewer of Europe'[9]. Our rapid burning of accumulated fuels is causing the carbon dioxide content of the air to rise steadily: there appears to be some dispute as to whether this will raise the world's temperature (thus melting the polar ice-caps, raising the sea's level by some sixty feet, and drowning the world's coastal cities) or lower it (thus introducing a new Ice Age)[10]. If it reaches toxic levels, we may not be around to discover which of these two prophecies was the more accurate. Meanwhile, London's atmosphere is so corrosive that Cleopatra's Needle suffered more damage in the last ninety years of its existence than in the first three thousand[11]. Plastic bottles and blobs of oil are found far out in the lonely ocean[12], and the Los Angeles smog can be seen (by astronauts) from twenty-five thousand miles away[13]. In 1969, a river in Ohio caught fire and burned two bridges down: it was full of volatile industrial discharges[14]. In New York, noise regularly reaches the level that leads directly to deafness[15]; and in California, children are regularly forbidden to play energetically or take exercise at school, since this would make them breathe more deeply.

Such news-items are commonplace today, and they add up to a problem that needs to be taken very seriously: responsible studies and surveys, undertaken by well-informed individuals and agencies, confirm the complex danger and the urgency of the problem. We are faced with something more than a loss of the simple goodness that earlier societies may or may not have possessed: we are threatened with something worse than a hideous destruction of rural and natural amenity. On the most optimistic assessment, we face a whole complex of environmental and ecological disasters; and while most of us will quite possibly survive them, there is no certainty even of this. Our case may be terminal: in so far as we are now repenting, we may be repenting too late. At this present time, there are responsible men—not only eccentrics in beards and homespun, but grave and cautious scientists as well—who ask in all seriousness whether *homo sapiens* can survive much longer. Other species have died out: ours may, and not necessarily by reason of a third world war.

In most of us, dramatic and terrible prognostications of this kind will probably breed an initial scepticism. There have been comparable scares before now, prophecies of doom, and vibrant calls to repentance which usually appeared to fall on deaf ears; and yet the human race has managed to stagger along somehow, managing its affairs very imperfectly and suffering a great deal of unnecessary trouble, but surviving.

Is this just another scare? There have certainly been comparable scares in the past, any number of them, and it was antecedently likely that there would be another at this particular time. An era, a millennium is drawing to its close, and this fact touches the imagination profoundly, on eschatological lines. They say that during the period that preceded the year 1000, Europe was charged with an expectation of Doomsday and the end; and it was perhaps to be expected that some people would respond in similar fashion to the approach of the year 2000. Their burning sincerity would be obvious enough, and so would the basically pathological nature of their anxiety.

Among those who utter these present warnings most loudly, there are certainly some whose manner and idiom invite an interpretation more or less of that kind. More generally, there are many who quite obviously relish the environmental crisis, because it gives them such a splendid pretext for hot-gospelling and denunciation. "Woe to the wicked city!" Cries of that kind are agreeable to utter, and they always attract an audience.

The sceptic's argument could be taken a stage further, on these slightly personal lines. Environmental worries appear to be felt most acutely—or at least, expressed most vociferously—in the United States; and in the psychology of that country, there are elements that might dispose people to an exaggerated emotionalism in this kind of connection. Up to a point, America has been shaped by the faith in progress, in technological development and industrial dynamism. But its mind has also been haunted, and powerfully, by the contrary myth. Energetically repudiating everything 'primitive', in the spirit of Hobbes, it also cherishes a nostalgic dream of primal simplicity and innocence, implanted there from the origins, notably by the influence of Rousseau—the pastoral dream of an Eden-continent, green and fertile, where a godly race of small farmers might live by Jeffersonian democracy and a stable sober sufficiency: Walden Pond and the virgin prairie. The American mind tends to be polarised between these two myths or visions[16], more sharply than has been usual in Europe, where it has been easier at least to believe in a balance or synthesis; and if Americans now cry out loudly at their own country's defiling of Nature, the subconscious power of that pastoral myth may give to their cries an urgency beyond what is warranted by the pure facts.

If so, they will still be responding in a very human and honourable way. "Deep in our hearts", says Dr. René Dubos[17], "we still personalize natural forces and for this reason experience guilt at their desecration. The manifestations of Nature are identified with unchangeable needs of human life and are charged with primeval emotions because man is still of the earth earthy."

While respecting such sentiments, the hard-headed sceptic may perhaps distrust the practical objectivity of those who feel them strongly; and his suspicions will be deeper where the passions involved are politically tinted.

In April 1970, a special day—'Earth Day'—was set aside for nation-wide protests and demonstrations, intended to make Americans more conscious of the environmental crisis and threat; and the motives behind this occasion were called in question on political lines. "A few rightists noted darkly that Earth Day was also Lenin's birthday, and warned that the entire happening was a Communist trick" [18]. To the rightists in question, of course, practically everything is a Communist trick. But then, and at other times, it did seem that certain individuals were active and vocal in environmental matters chiefly because they were thereby given a new basis for attacking American capitalism and American industry and the American way of life generally. As in the comparable issue of war and violence, indignation often seemed to be politically selective. It could work the other way round: certain people on the political left asserted angrily that the whole environmental problem had been staged and inflated by the establishment in order to distract Americans from the real issues of war and race.

No argument is refuted, of course, by any demonstration that those who advance it are impurely motivated: environmental fears might be whipped up for political reasons by the right or the left or both, and still be completely justified in fact. But a pinch of salt is always good medicine; and it needs to be remembered that while it has now become fashionable to express dark fears about the future of technological man, there are many well-informed people who take a more cheerful view and rebuke the alarmists. "Men have become like Gods", says Dr. Edmund Leach[19]; "Isn't it about time that we understood our divinity? Science offers us total mastery over our environment and over our destiny, yet instead of rejoicing we feel deeply afraid. Why should this be? . . . Why do so many of us talk as if the advancing sweep of technology were a natural catastrophe beyond all human control?"

Dr. Leach does not write as a religious man, and many

Christians might see this as an alarmingly hubristic way of talking, a specimen of how the human mind behaves when it forgets the limitations of mankind and proudly courts disaster. It is therefore noteworthy that a very similar kind of language could be spoken by one whom many regard as the foremost religious genius of the century. "The dream which human research obscurely fosters," wrote Teilhard de Chardin[20], "is fundamentally that of mastering . . . the ultimate energy of which all other energies are merely servants; and thus, by grasping the very mainspring of evolution, seizing the tiller of the world." He continued: "I salute those who have the courage to admit that their hopes extend that far; they are at the pinnacle on mankind; and I would say to them that there is less difference than people think between research and adoration."

We are far indeed, here, from the pessimism of the American[21] who recently said: "Nothing we can do will keep humankind in existence for as long as another two centuries." Teilhard de Chardin went so far as to assert— on theoretical grounds—that human history could not *possibly* come to any kind of catastrophic end [22]. He expected, instead, "a maturation and a paroxysm leading ever higher into the Improbable from which we have sprung" [23].

While various views can plausibly be taken of the probable human future, the extremes of optimism and pessimism do strain credulity a little. Teilhard's rhapsodical confidence seems ill-founded by any kind of criterion, scientific or theological; on the other hand, one can retain a certain scepticism about its converse. Environmental fears can be over-dramatised. The human race will hardly continue in temporal existence for ever: sooner or later, it must die out or be destroyed, and it is quite possible that we shall cause ourselves to be destroyed. A nuclear war and the consequent fall-out could do the job completely and quickly. But any other tendency towards the corporate suicide of our race might prove to be self-limiting. The activities that create the environmental danger are among the characteristic activities of a populous and highly-organised society, prosperous and active in technological and industrial developments: even an ordinary trade recession would slow them down, and they might be expected to grind to a standstill if wholesale mortality were to set in for any reason, bringing with it a high degree of social and technical and industrial disruption. Death might succeed where prudence had failed: long before the whole three-and-a-half thousand million of us had died, the survivors might be obliged to abandon the activities that had caused the trouble.

This is cold and doubtful comfort at the best. Let us cherish whatever optimism we can: there remains the certainty—amply supported by scientific evidence, and constantly emphasised by people who cannot possibly be dismissed as mere alarmists—that technological man is most unlikely to continue for very much longer on his present course. Disaster—less than total, perhaps, but quite disastrous enough—seems certain to come upon us before long: only for a short time can we continue to enjoy the present quantity and quality of our living.

Exaggerated things are certainly being said here and there. But in general, the environmental and ecological crisis is a real one, a serious danger, by no means a scare or fantasy. "Man feels threatened and *is* threatened by the estrangement of life from the conditions and natural cycles under which human evolution occurred; by the constant and unavoidable exposure to the stimuli of urban and industrial civilisation; by the varied aspects of environmental pollution; by the emotional trauma and often the solitude of life in congested cities; by the monotony, the boredom, indeed, the compulsory leisure ensuing from automated work" [24]. Technological man has reached a turning-point: he needs to re-consider his situation, his policy, his habitual structure of priorities and values.

All times, notoriously, are times of transition. But not all times have that character equally. Now and again, the general flux of history becomes for a short while exceptionally rapid and more fundamental: there are points at which changed circumstances and changed outlooks will cause any society to embark cumbrously upon a radical change of direction.

It seems that we live nowadays at such a moment. There are a great many revolutionary sentiments and radical questionings in the air, and these can be analysed variously, with diverse assessments of the probable outcome. But one thing is fairly clear: whereas most of us assumed in the past that our world was going to become more and more technological—presumably for ever—and was likely to thrive on that basis, we now find this prospect much less credible and also much less attractive.

It used to provide an orthodoxy. Perhaps thirty-five years ago, one would often find in some popular magazine "our artist's impression of London in the year 2035." The drawing would show a towering rectilinear townscape, all concrete and chromium, grim and functional, with sleek transportation arrowing madly in all directions: a machine-city, with mankind—usually clad, for some reason, in shiny plastic tights—living in hygienic humourless subordination to the steel efficiency of the hive. The idea was that we should welcome this prospect with awe and submission, and thus display our loyalty to the modern age and the future.

Having already moved some distance in that kind of direction, we now see that picture as a hellish one, and implausible too. Our present-day sketch of 2035 would more probably show a few savages, scuffling and scratching for food among the ruins. The confident progress of _homo techno-scientificus_ turns out to be taking us towards disaster, and by a route that lacks even the dangerous charm of the primrose path.

Some kind of a reappraisal, or change of heart and direction, is necessary and is already under way, though incoherently. From the current awareness of this necessity, we can derive a certain comfort. Changed motivations and values—coupled, perhaps, with an economic recession—might lead to a slowing-down of our present technomaniac frenzy, and thus to a natural easing of the environmental crisis, in some of its aspects at least. Dr. Dubos hopes[25] for "the emergence of a grass-roots movement, powered by romantic emotion as much as by factual knowledge, that will give form and strength to the latent public concern with environmental quality." An inchoate movement of that kind is already in existence, and it may—quite possibly—resist the obvious temptation to develop in a Nazi direction. It must certainly be combative, since it is up against "the colossal inertia and rigidity—if not indifference—of social and academic institutions" [26].

But it would be rash to place great trust in the wisdom of viscerally-governed mass movements. Clear thinking is as necessary as strong feeling: over-simplification is a constant danger, and energies can easily be dissipated in the castigation of approximately-chosen scapegoats. One cannot simply say that 'technology' or 'industry' or 'business' is the enemy, and devise a revolution accordingly. As Gabriel Marcel said some years ago[27], "It would indeed be to fall under the joint spells of sentimentalism and ideology to hope for some sort of Gandhi revolution and a return to a pre-technical age. The burden of technics has been assumed by man and he can no longer put it down because he finds it heavy."

On the other hand, if technology creates problems, it would be extremely rash to assume that further technology will solve them. Despite recent doubts, this assumption is still made by many, perhaps by the great majority: the faith of *homo techno-scientificus* is deeply rooted by now, and the consequent habit of mind has great momentum. A generation that has put a man on the moon will not easily lose its technical self-confidence merely because—say—the atmosphere has become dangerously polluted. Initially at least, it will see here a new challenge to its own distinctive kind of ingenuity.

Up to a point, this kind of response to the environmental crisis still makes sense. In the fashion of a technological society, we are perfectly well able to be technically clever about all manner of particular problems and difficulties, once these have been isolated and defined. If some local disaster seems to threaten, we can think of something in the nature of a local remedy; we can devise some method of controlling this particular kind of pollution, or conserving that particular element in our total resources.

But however unfamiliar and unwelcome the idea may be, we need to accept the increasingly obvious fact that this approach to the problem has its limitations. For one thing, human nature is rather reluctant to make sacrifices in the common interest. Environmental difficulties arise from activities that offer short-term benefits against long-term dangers; if they are to be technically and governmentally mastered, the operation will demand from all of us a greater degree of foresight and of moral nobility than it seems realistic to expect. "Keeping streets and houses clear of refuse, filtering and chlorinating the water supplies, watching over the purity of food products, assuring a safe minimum of fresh air in public places constitute measures that can be applied by the collectivity without interfering seriously with individual freedom. These measures are readily accepted because they do not demand personal effort from their beneficiaries. In contrast, any measure that requires individual discipline is more likely to be neglected"[28]. Will the free citizens of London and New York freely renounce the petrol-driven vehicle for the sake of clean air? How many of us will consistently choose an expensive health-food diet for its dull wholesomeness, when the shops are full of cheap and varied and delicious foods that are said to be slightly polluted?

People do not always act in their own best interests, and cannot easily be made to do so. Technical mastery of the environmental crisis would involve a politically impossible degree of coercion, exercised over the public at large and —especially—over commercial interests that would put up a stiff fight.

It would also be weak on credibility. If one thing has emerged clearly from recent studies of the crisis, it is the tendency for particular solutions to breed new problems, equally threatening and intractable or more so. "If technology got man into this mess, surely technology can get him out of it again. Not necessarily, argues Anthony Wiener of the Hudson Institute. Wiener sees technological man as the personification of Faust, endlessly pursuing the unattainable. 'Our bargain with the Devil', he says, 'is that we will figure out the consequences of whatever we do. We may have a 100% probability of solving all those problems as they arise. But as we solve them, we may find that our only remedies will create more of the same problems'.[29] "

"What shall we do?" asks Dr. Lynn White Jr.[30]; "No one yet knows. Unless we think about fundamentals, our specific measures may produce backlashes more serious than those they are intended to remedy." This seems to apply, not only to panic-measures taken in a crisis, but to the whole process by which we seek our well-being on elaborately technological lines. "Abundance of goods, excess of comfort, multiplicity of means of communication are generating in the modern world situations almost as distressing as the ones that used to result from shortages of food, painful physical labour, and social isolation. We are creating new problems in the very process of solving those which plagued humanity in the past"[31]. Dr. Dubos is here thinking of medical problems: by seeking his own well-being on technomaniac lines, modern man is making himself literally ill, and seriously.

The cleverness of *homo techno-scientificus* is a remarkable thing, in itself and in its achievements, and despite all these misgivings, it has done great things for the human race. But it is not an absolute, and it cannot solve all problems. "An implicit and almost universal assumption of discussions published in professional and semipopular scientific journals is that the problem under discussion has a technical solution," observes Mr. Garrett Hardin[32]; and he continues, "the concern here is with the important concept of a class of human problems which can be called 'no technical solution problems'." Apart from palliative measures here and there, it seems that the environmental problem falls into that category.

But it would be a mistake—though, to some people, a tempting one—to go to the other extreme and denounce mere 'technology' as the villain of the piece. It cannot be wholly to blame. The environmental problem is a new one, whereas we have always been 'technological' in some degree, and for the most part, quite harmlessly. Even now, most of it does little harm. The trouble arises not from our old tendency to have technologies and improve them wherever possible, but rather from our new tendency to look upon technique as an end in itself, an absolute, to be pursued for its own sake. It is only a means; and as Charles Williams said [33], "When the means are autonomous, they are deadly."

We can thus speak, precisely enough, of technomania; we can detect in our society an almost pathological tendency to confer autonomy upon all technical methods and means, and in the environmental crisis we can see the consequent deadliness at work. The trouble arises, perhaps, because we are vague about ends: living in a fragmented culture, we suffer from the lack of any coherent system of value and purpose in human life. We are clever at travelling, but we are quite at a loss—collectively—when it comes to the question of evaluating one possible destination as against another: we concentrate, therefore, upon the mechanisms of mere travel. Chesterton once described ours as the age which invented the loudspeaker and then found that it had nothing to say: our remedy is to build larger and noisier loudspeakers. "The huge multiplication of means put at man's disposal," says Gabriel Marcel [34], "takes place at the cost of the ends they are supposed to serve, or, if you like, at the cost of the values which man is called upon both to serve and to safeguard. It is as if man, overburdened by the weight of technics, knows less and less where he stands in regard to what matters to him and what doesn't, to what is precious and what is worthless."

Thus bewildered, we comfort and reassure ourselves by concentrating our attention upon what we understand best, the technical means; and many of us derive great solace from the fact that technique—unlike life in general—is a field in which something like perfection can actually be achieved. But the ends are too difficult for us; or perhaps, we are embarrassed by the painful questions that any serious consideration of ends and purposes and value would raise. We hope, therefore, that if we drive fast enough, in a sufficiently new and astonishing machine, the excitement will distract our attention from the sad certainty that we don't really know where we are going, or why, and that we aren't enjoying the journey as much as we expected, and seem rather likely to have a bad accident.

The fact is that something has gone seriously wrong with the relationship between twentieth-century man and his environment, and between his means and his ends. We are therefore mis-using this world horribly. This is something over and above the general imperfection of human existence; and we have started to worry about it, at the practical and theoretical levels alike, but uncertainly.

It is suggested now that if we are baffled by the environmental problem, it is because of a general failure to see it in context and to recognise the kind of problem that it is. Fundamentally, it is not a problem of the empirical and technical kind that our positivistic society handles with the greatest confidence and the greatest hope of success. It goes deeper than that. It concerns the ultimate rock-bottom relationship between man and the world, and the doctrines that we believe and also the semi-conscious assumptions that we make about that relationship. To a greater degree than modern secular man can easily or willingly recognise, it therefore has the character of a 'religious' problem, as against—say—a technical or governmental kind of problem. "What people do about their ecology," says Dr. Lynn White Jr.[35], "depends upon what they think about themselves in relation to things around them. Human ecology is deeply conditioned by beliefs about our nature and destiny

—that is, by religion." If you consider ends rather than means, if you embark upon any radical worrying about how humanity stands in relation to the world, you are raising a question of the specific kind that the various religions and theologies of mankind have attempted—in their different ways, and with whatever kind of success—to answer.

But we of the twentieth century are not altogether happy with religious questions, and we tend therefore to overlook or evade the essentially religious nature of our environmental difficulties. We do not want the problem to have that embarrassing and unmanageable nature: instinctively, we tend to coerce it into the kind of pattern or category that we already understand and can handle with confidence. We try, in fact, to make it into a problem of that technical and governmental kind, so that we can then hope to deal with it by new techniques and new plans and new regulations, comparable to those that did so much for us in the past.

This instinct appears to be very widespread. The environmental problem is a familiar one by now, a subject of everyday discussion; and when such a discussion is well under way, somebody will usually break out with an impatient cry of "But what can we *do*?" At such a time, questioning will usually make it clear that the speaker is thinking on those *activiste* lines: he assumes that the situation can and should be met by some kind of outward 'doing', technical in its subject-matter, governmental or international in its planning and enforcement. Are we threatened by environmental and ecological disaster? Then let us devise new techniques or modify old ones; let there be laws, strictly enforced by authority, imposing limitations upon what we do and how we do it. Thus, collectively, we shall *master* the situation!

This book proposes to explore the mutual relevance between Christian theology and the environmental crisis; and the starting-point of its argument is a conviction that this natural *activisme* will hardly do. It is doubtfully realistic and grossly insufficient. At the best, it proposes a nibbling at fringes and symptoms; at the clearly probable worst, it proposes a further large dose of what originally caused the disease; throughout, it ignores the nature of the problem.

Marginally and in particular contexts, we undoubtedly do need certain new techniques and new regulations. But very much more seriously and radically, our society has another need—one that can only be expressed in dreadfully old-fashioned language. We need to repent of a heresy.

Two

⁑

If something has gone seriously and radically wrong with the relationship between twentieth-century man and his environment, we shall need to re-think that relationship as fundamentally and precisely as we can. We shall need to get our ideas straight: that is to say, we shall need to be 'orthodox' in something like the literal sense of that word. And if this environmental problem does indeed have a basically religious character, the more specialised kind of orthodoxy may also be relevant. Let it be supposed that Christianity is 'true', in some sense that may perhaps be elusive: even so, we shall only get the benefit of its truth in so far as we understand it correctly, avoiding those confusions and distortions that were—in the crudely dogmatic past—called 'heresies'.

If that word 'heresy' distresses us, with its suggestion of intolerance and the Inquisition, we can use the alternative word coined by Dr. Sam Keen[1]—'ideopathology', a pathological condition of our outlook or ideology. But this should not be necessary: we should not be frightened of the word 'heresy' when it is used (as in this book) with no suggestion at all that the heretic ought to be silenced or burned at the stake. The fear of dogmatism, and therefore of words associated with dogmatism, can be taken to neurotic lengths. In their desire to be tolerant, in their anxiety to respect and accommodate all views, some people talk as though religion were a field within which no man could ever be simply mistaken—or, perhaps, one in which it was somehow unimportant to get things right. This is an absurd view: nobody would dream of applying it to any other field of possible knowledge. Rightness, in religious matters, may be impossible: it can hardly be undesirable. One can be a sceptic, and deny all possibility of religious knowledge: one can be a logical positivist, and find no meaning in religious discourse. But if religion is—in any sense at all—a field of knowledge, it is also a field in which ignorance and error can be present, and (there as elsewhere) undesirable.

With this *apologia*, with this explanation of the terminology used, our theme can be outlined. This book is an enquiry into the relationship between two things: the present-day environmental crisis on the one hand, and on the other, the traditional teaching of Christianity about the material universe. At first sight, these might appear to be unrelated subjects: it is suggested that there is a close connection between them, and in particular, that our environmental troubles amount to one consequence and symptom of an old consistent tendency in religion, a false cult or heresy by Christian standards, an outlook of great historical importance, widely prevalent in our society today but seldom recognised.

This theme can perhaps be approached most usefully by a consideration of the various options that are available, if one tries to work out a basic religious attitude towards this world—'Nature', the phenomenal universe, the environment. There are not a great many possibilities; and of these, only three are directly relevant to Western thinking.

In the first place, one can believe that this world was created by a fallen angel or an evil spirit, or something of that kind, and is therefore a bad thing in itself—a prison, perhaps, in which we are most unfortunately trapped. With any view of this kind, there will naturally be associated a corresponding emotional and imaginative habit, of distrust and hostility towards the world of daily experience; and it will mean very little to ask how far this was the cause, and how far the consequence, of the abstract or propositional belief. The two things can only be separated out by a somewhat artificial kind of analysis: psychologically, and especially in the key medium of myth, they are one.

This view of the world has been held by a great many high-minded and deeply religious people: it is of immense historical importance for the West, a most powerful determinant of our culture. The curious thing is that during these last few centuries, it has quite ceased to be present in Western society as a conscious and admitted theology, an organised body of doctrine. Its continued presence and power, at a deeper psychological level, is the principal theme of this book.

In the second place, we can dissociate the question of this world's origin and nature from any question of divinity or supernatural power, evil or good. This planet and the entire universe will then be seen in totally non-religious terms, though lip-service may still be paid to a remote and theoretical God. The sense of creation will not be strong: things will seem to have evolved automatically, mechanically, by the blind operation of natural law, and an attitude of neutrality or indifference towards them will seem appropriate and may be psychologically inescapable. It will seem that the universe is neither good nor evil in itself: it is merely *there*, not to be despised, not to be revered. We may respond to it emotionally; but if so, this will only be a psychological and physiological and sociological fact about ourselves. There will be no possibility of supposing that any particular response to the universe is objectively appropriate.

In the third place, one can believe that this world is the handiwork of a good and loving Creator, and his dearly-loved personal property as well. When fully believed, this idea will be associated with an instinctive tendency to venerate and cherish this world, to handle it with caution and care and respect, as a thing immensely good in its own right, quite apart from its possible usefulness to ourselves. Any failure to make this kind of response will seem like a failure in objectivity and realism, as well as in piety.

This view of the world is, of course, familiar to all of us, in principle if not in lived experience: it is the officially central doctrine of the Judaeo-Christian tradition, within which—or within the vestiges of which—most of us were reared. It is the basis of all religion, as most of us understand that word. At the very beginning of the Bible and at the very end, we find it asserted: Genesis tells us emphatically that God created all things, and—most repetitively—that he found them positively good, even before man came along to enjoy them[2]; and similarly, at the very end of the story, "Thou hast created all things, and for thy pleasure they are, and were created"[3]. In a secondary sense they were made for man; but man, lord of creation in a limited way, is still part of it, materially one with the dust of the earth, united with the rest of creation in serving uncreated purpose, in existing to delight God, and in possessing therefore a quality of inherent and wonderful goodness. All things are holy, ourselves included. Throughout the Old Testament, but especially in the Psalms[4] and the

Book of Job[5], this note is sounded again and again—a note of delight and celebration before the greatness of the Creator and the goodness, the holiness of his visible works: a sentiment which "links every being, every event to God, without miracle and almost without mystery, in such a way that to a Jew all things are sacred, all things sacrament" [6].

This lyricism, this *excitement* about the goodness of God's creation was the natural and almost the logical consequence of Jewish monotheism; and it carried over into Christianity, rather erratically at the level of popular sentiment, but vigorously at the level of doctrine. In the gospel, we hear that God cares intensely about the destiny of birds and flowers; in the creeds, we find it stated explicitly that all things were made by a benevolent Father, and their consequent goodness is implied clearly enough. The theologians never doubted it: the whole concept of Incarnation and then of sacrament presupposed it. St Augustine, having passed some time under the influence of a very different philosophy, came to assert robustly that God made all things positively good, so that the word 'bad' can only refer to a deprivation of good [7]. St Thomas Aquinas declared that God's purpose in creation was the communication of his own goodness, in which his creatures participate by reason of their existence and in the measure of it[8]. And all down the Christian centuries, the same idea was asserted again and again, in the treatises of theologians and in the pronouncements of church authorities: those who denied it (as many did) tended to incur the full anger of the ecclesiastical machine and of the associated secular arm.

This idea is part of our inheritance, and not only on the Judaeo-Christian side: Aristotle had asserted the goodness of all being, merely as such[9]; Plato had groped towards the idea of a single beneficent Creator[10]; Stoic monism went so far as to equate the universe with the divine perfection. The very word *cosmos*, in Greek, was not a merely neutral or descriptive term: it carried within itself a heavy emotional loading, a note of admiration and approval for the order and goodness and beauty of this world [11].

Such ideas recur throughout the whole Judaeo-Christian-Hellenic way of thinking, constituting the first and most basic dogma of the religious system that we inherit. It seems possible that present-day Christians—and their adversaries as well—pay to this fundamental doctrine rather less attention than it deserves. Perhaps it is too familiar, perhaps it seems too obvious: some people certainly talk as though it were a truism—as though, given only a generally 'religious' approach to the universe, this doctrine of God's creation and of his creation's goodness then followed quite easily and inevitably.

It does not: there are plausible and very different alternatives, towards which (if one is unaware of them) one can gravitate quite unconsciously. The Christian view of the phenomenal universe is very far from being a truism: it is much more like a dogmatic and daring paradox, and if it is true, it is a truth to which men only cling with difficulty.

It can seem immensely and wonderfully plausible from time to time. "God's in his heaven—All's right with the world!" With these words in mind, people have sometimes seen fit to castigate Browning for a fatuously Panglossian kind of optimism, a crude unawareness of evil. They should pay closer attention to the highly ironical functioning, in its context, of Pippa's song.

But she does express one element in our experience. From time to time—often, if we are fortunate—we are as-

saulted suddenly by an overwhelming intuition of goodness, a gust of warm approval and love towards this dear
and happy world, and of gratitude towards its Creator.
Notoriously, it is at such moments that the atheist is poor-
est: he has nobody to thank. But he is eased before long.
The mood soon passes: it had its own causality, psychological or glandular.

But while the mood—as such—can be explained away,
there remains an obstinate suspicion that it corresponded
somehow with some kind of reality. Such moments, when
remembered, do not have the flavour of illusion: they suggest, rather, a sudden access of vision or objectivity,
clouded over too rapidly by the returning fog of habit.
Happier circumstances or the right kind of mental discipline might possibly make the vision permanent, and this
—we feel—would be a gain in realism.

Such moments come to everybody. However teasingly,
however uncertainly, each man shares at times in the intuitional belief, the hope that when the chips are down, this
creation *deserves* to be appreciated and loved without mis-
giving. "Something tells him that the ultimate idea of a
world is not bad or even neutral; staring at the sky or the
grass or the truths of mathematics or even a new-laid egg,
he has a vague feeling like the shadow of that saying of the
great Christian philosopher, St Thomas Aquinas, 'Every
existence, as such, is good'.[12]"

If one stared always at skies and grasses and mathematical truths and new-laid eggs, the case would be simple. But from time to time, one is likely to be staring at
something less agreeable—let us say, at a child dying of
leukaemia: one's own child, perhaps.

Intuition works both ways: however we assess its authority, it tells conflicting stories. Let it be granted that we
often experience what seems to be a direct awareness of

this world's goodness and (by implication) of the Creator's love. But at other times—more often, if we are unlucky—we are assaulted by just the opposite kind of experience: one that seems to have exactly the same credentials, exactly the same plaus'bility, but a very different content. At such a moment this world can seem malevolent, hostile, evil: perhaps more unhappily still, it can seem utterly cold and blind and indifferent. Either way, the experience makes pure falsity and self-deception out of those other sentiments that we felt when we stared so happily at the sky and the grass. "What most 'nature poets' are apt to forget," said Aldous Huxley[13], "is that the immediately apprehended quality of things is not invariably a quality of supernatural beauty: it is also, on occasions, a quality of supernatural evil, supernatural ugliness. And even the loveliness is sometimes supernaturally remote and uncaring."

Is 'Nature' really friendly, really admirable? Is the universe on our side? Is it really a good thing, made and cherished by a God of unlimited power who is also pure love? Does it bear any obvious hall-mark of benevolent omnipotence at work?

In certain moods at least, we can see it very differently —perhaps as a kind of hell, perhaps merely as a botched and amateurish job. We can all sympathise with the Spanish king who said: "Had I been present at the creation, I would have given some useful hints for the better ordering of the universe."

One certainly can take the more positive view—especially if one is well-fed and in good health, financially comfortable, not bereaved, adapted to circumstances and to oneself, selective in one's awareness, and nicely accommodated in a temperate climate. But let there be a slight change in one's condition, a slight shift in one's perspective, and a very different assessment of the universe will crash in upon the mind: a sharply negative assessment, such as was put forward by C. S. Lewis[14] to explain his one-time disbelief in God. "Look at the universe we live in," he began. "By far the greatest part of it consists of empty space, completely dark and unimaginably cold." "In this universe", he continued, "life is a casual by-product, a matter of chance and then chiefly of suffering, especially where human life is concerned; and it is doomed. Every race that comes into being in any part of the universe is doomed; for the universe, they tell us, is running down, and will sometime be a uniform infinity of homogeneous matter at a low temperature. All stories will come to nothing: all life will turn out in the end to have been a transitory and senseless contortion upon the idiotic face of infinite matter. If you ask me to believe that this is the work of a benevolent and omnipotent spirit, I reply that all the evidence points in the opposite direction. Either there is no spirit behind the universe, or else a spirit indifferent to good and evil, or else an evil spirit."

The goodness of our universe is not obvious. At times we seem to feel it. But at other times we feel the opposite; and there are long periods in most lives during which it seems almost meaningless to attribute either goodness or badness to the universe. It is simply, wearily *there*.

Some people talk loosely as though, from experienced goodness and happiness, one could make a direct inference to the existence of something like the Christian God. On the face of things at least, it seems that this kind of argument cuts both ways: on just the same basis, from experienced evil and misery, one could infer the existence of a Satan or something more than a Satan, an uncreated counter-God or Ahriman of evil.

Is this universe perhaps ruled by two powers, of light and of darkness? Are they perhaps in contest, with a great no-man's-land between them, a large area of flat and neutral experience, possessed by neither?

At the intuitional level, such a view might be considered to make more obvious sense than the paradoxical view of the Christians. And if, from these rather subjective approaches, we turn to stricter reasoning, we may be dismayed by the cogency of the arguments commonly and easily brought against the Christian view. The agnostic hardly needs to be hostile: he can afford to be quite gentle and sympathetic, so inescapably lucid his case appears to be. The Christian attributes both omnipotence and benevolence to a single God, and he views the world accordingly: the agnostic replies that he can accept the idea of a God in principle, and also the idea that this God might be *either* omnipotent *or* benevolent. But he is logically baffled by the idea that God has both qualities: it seems quite incompatible with experience.

At painful moments, the argument has come home to both of us. There is no need to survey the whole sad cruel universe: the case is proved sufficiently by that one instance, of a small child dying in pain. His smallness is to be stressed: not in order to harrow the heart, but in order to by-pass the question of guilt and punishment. If you or I die in pain, we may possibly deserve it: that question at least arises, to complicate the issue. But not even the strictest moralist will say this of a two-year-old.

Here he is, then, and dying: what are we to say to the mother? Could God have prevented this? Can he now cure the child by miracle? The dilemma seems absolute. If God is unable to prevent or cure, he cannot be called omnipotent: his power has met with insurmountable opposition, coming perhaps from that evil counter-God, or from some intractability in the nature of things. If (on the other hand) God can remedy this situation but chooses not to, his power will not be in doubt; but in this case, his goodness, his fatherly love will hardly be credible unless words are to lose all normal meaning.

We seem to be left with the theoretical possibility of a single God who is either all-powerful or all-loving, but not —conceivably—both; and things are not much helped by the Christian apologist who now rushes in to explain that God permits suffering, on a temporary basis, so that disproportionately greater blessings can be conferred in the future. This only takes the argument one stage further back. Is God compelled to achieve his excellent purposes in this cruel way? If so, his omnipotence goes. Or is this what he *chooses*? If so, how can we call him 'Father'? In the spirit of love, an earthly father may think it necessary to punish his sons for their own ultimate good; but only because this is a harsh world, not of his making. He would prefer it if there were no such necessity, but an earthly father does not command all things. How do we judge a father who, commanding all things in absolute power, still allows that necessity to remain?

For the Christian, the moral problem of evil is a thorny one, intellectually and emotionally as well: to even the firmest of believers, there comes a moment when the goodness of the Creator—and therefore of his work—loses all credibility. The universe becomes a nightmare and God a kind of devil, hating and tormenting mankind, deriding our grief:

> "As flies to wanton boys are we to the gods,
> They kill us for their sport" [15].

At such a time, Promethean defiance will seem the only possible, the only *decent* response to the whole religious problem:

> "We for a certainty are not the first
>   Have sat in taverns while the tempest hurled
> Their hopeful plans to emptiness, and cursed
>   Whatever brute and blackguard made the world" [16].

And then, in our calmer moments, a sly philosophical voice intrudes to remind us of the second or metaphysical problem of evil. If God's will is the foundation of all being, how can anything possibly 'be' *against* the will of God? How can sin and evil be meaningfully said to exist at all? It helps very little if we define evil in negative terms, as *privatio boni* or as mere illusion. Once again, this only takes the argument one stage further back: we have to admit that privation and illusion are themselves evil, and this leaves us where we started.

Does the Christian view of the universe really make sense? Does it not seem like a foolish attempt to cling to two contradictory ideas? If we must believe in a God and his goodness, would it not be more realistic to admit that his power is plainly limited?—that there exists also some kind of a counter-God, our God's enemy, present and powerful in the world of our experience? Given that we are to speak in a broadly theistic kind of language, is this not the obvious answer? And is this not admitted—however cautiously—by Christian tradition, with all its ancient talk of Satan, the Prince of Darkness, the Prince of this world?

But defiantly, the faithful still shout: "I believe in *one* God, the Father Almighty". The agnostic shrugs his shoulders, as one confronted by mere obstinacy.

This is not a treatise on the twofold problem of evil. Our

present concern is with the difficulty—the *prima facie* absurdity, even—of the Christian view. It is certainly not a truism: it involves an apparent contradiction and certainly an extreme kind of paradox, an implied oxymoron, summed up (if paternity implies benevolence) in the opening words of either Creed.

Comfort is perhaps available: to some extent, the moral problem at least is a pseudo-problem, a verbal illusion, since it can hardly be stated—and has not been stated above—without gross violation of the grammatical laws that must necessarily govern all meaningful discourse about God. But even on the most favourable assessment, any simple assertion of the world's goodness and of the Creator's benevolence must represent an unfinished kind of philosophy. It demands completion. Whatever the strength of his intuitions, an intelligent man cannot simply celebrate the goodness of his environment and leave it at that. "He must either deny the existence of God, as all atheists do; or he must deny the present union between God and man, as all Christians do" [17].

Something like a doctrine of original sin therefore becomes necessary. If we start off by firmly attributing goodness to the one Creator and to his work, we shall have to add that this is a goodness very imperfectly embodied in our present human condition, very erratically perceived by ourselves. We are out of touch with it, estranged from it: something has gone wrong with us.

This will be an unwelcome conclusion. The Fall of Man is not a very popular doctrine nowadays. For one thing, it cuts right across the evolutionary habit of the modern imagination, our intense desire to see all things (our own history especially) in terms of steady improvement. And apart from this, it makes some of us theologically nervous. Christianity has not really recovered yet from the traumatic events of the nineteenth century—the triumph of science, the discomfiture of Bishop Wilberforce before Thomas Henry Huxley, the headlong dishevelled retreat from crude fundamentalism. The relevant nerves remain raw and sensitive: even now, we suspect that if we raise the question of Original Sin, we shall be met with a sardonic grin and a certain amount of jocularity about Adam and Eve, the garden, the serpent, the apple, the fig-leaves. We tend to be bashful about Genesis, just as though that pseudo-problem of the Victorian age still presented real intellectual difficulties for the Christian.

In other ways, too, the doctrine of the Fall is unpalatable. It insults our sense of human splendour; where "the troubles of our proud and angry state" are concerned, it puts the blame squarely upon ourselves, when we would much prefer to blame God or destiny; by insisting that our social structures must always be built out of flawed material, it undermines various kinds of worldly hope.

On the other hand, it does seem to fit the facts: the whole texture of experience does suggest that something has gone seriously wrong with the human race. "Whatever else men have believed," said Chesterton[18], "they have all believed that there is something the matter with mankind." The consensus is not in fact universal, but it is extensive and realistic: on the mere face of things, it seems that Newman may have been right in saying that our race was involved in some "aboriginal catastrophe". "The evidence," according to Arthur Koestler[19], "seems to indicate that at some point during the last explosive stages of the evolution of *homo sapiens*, something has gone wrong; that there is a flaw, some subtle engineering mistake built into our native equipment, which would account for the paranoid streak running through our history." It is a strictly human flaw: though Nature may be red in tooth and claw, the innocent brutes seem better organised, better behaved, less furiously at war with themselves and their environment. "Under normal conditions, in their natural habitats, wild animals do not mutilate themselves, masturbate, attack their offspring, develop stomach ulcers, become fetishists, suffer from obesity, form homosexual pair-bonds, or commit murder"[20].

The world is good enough, but we are born into a depraved species; and we can hardly complain, since each one of us quite freely casts his vote on the side of depravity again and again throughout his life. The heart is deceitful above all things, and desperately wicked: every prospect pleases, and only man is vile.

To some such unflattering conclusion are we drawn, and to a difficult theology and an exacting moral task, if we start off by accepting the Christian paradox about the goodness of the material universe and of its Creator.

Three

Can we possibly find some more acceptable approach to the whole question? One that involves us in fewer difficulties?

Mankind is certainly ill at ease, in a mess, very imperfectly at home in this universe. The Christians explain the fact by saying that we have abominably misused a good world. Could they be wrong? Would it be nearer the mark, perhaps, to choose another of our three initial options—to claim that we are relatively innocent, but have very unfortunately been trapped into an evil world?

The idea is plausible, and it is supported by a huge weight of human testimony: in so far as our thoughts and feelings tend in that direction, we shall be moving towards an association with one of the most ancient, persistent, and spiritual of all religious systems. We may even be joining the majority. Outside the Judaeo-Christian tradition, the strong belief in one creating God, and in the positive goodness of his creation and of our existence, has not come at all naturally or universally to religious man. In other traditions, and especially in Asia, he has very often tended to look upon the visible universe as illusory or insignificant or evil, and to see the present human condition as inherently unfortunate or disastrous to some degree. Matter (he feels) is relatively or totally bad: goodness can only be attributed to spirit, and the religious task is essentially one of transcending this world, helping spirit to rise above its material clog and defilement.

This view makes an obvious kind of sense, and it has always appealed strongly to high-minded and sensitive people—more especially when circumstances have been adverse, discouraging the easier kinds of optimism. It is, perhaps, the natural religion of mankind, once the primitive or animistic stage has been passed: it offers the first and the most obvious answer to the dark problem of good and evil.

It is, however, quite incompatible with orthodox Christianity: it clashes not only with the doctrine of God's creation, but also with any idea of Incarnation, of sacrament, and of the body's resurrection. Even so, it has played a most important part in the religious history of the Christian West; and the curious thing is that in our common vocabulary of the present day, there exists no generally-understood name for this large and distinct element in our collective past, this perennial tendency in the human mind. There are names, certainly, for the various local and temporary movements in which it has been embodied from time to time. But these are known chiefly to scholars and students. The average educated man knows roughly what a Catholic is, a Protestant, a Communist, a Flat-Earther; but he would be somewhat puzzled if you claimed to detect a Dualistic, Gnostic, Manichaean, Albigensian, Paulician, Bogomil, or Catharist element in his way of thinking.

There should be a distinctive but general name for the very characteristic outlook that consistently comes into being, whenever men combine a belief in God with a denial of this world's goodness.

It is an important outlook, a most powerful influence upon our own past and our present as well. In various forms and under many curious names—some of these have just been mentioned—it crops up again and again throughout European history, commonly as an influence from the East (usually mediated through the Balkans), but also arising spontaneously in this place and that. Sometimes it has been an institutional rival to the Christian and Catholic Church, a frankly alternative faith, a different religion: quite as widely, it has existed as an undefinable tendency within that Church, a semi-articulate heresy, an enemy within the gates. It has often managed, therefore, to become confused with orthodox Christianity. People will sometimes tell you (for example) that Christians —and Catholics in particular—look upon sex with basic disapproval, as though it were inherently evil, despite a very clear statement to the contrary in Genesis, and despite the official Catholic doctrine that sexual reproduction (*matrimonium*) is a sacrament, an especially holy thing. There could hardly be a more total mistake. That negative view of sex is precisely and distinctively true of this heresy, this alternative religion: individuals have often sympathised with it, but the Church as a whole has fought it very consistently down the centuries, sometimes by preaching and argument, and sometimes by the more questionable methods of crusade and persecution.

This outlook, this heresy needs a general name. For the purposes of this book, and in the full consciousness of oversimplification, it will be called 'Manichaeanism'. Strictly speaking, this word should only be used in connection with one particular version of it—the religious cult and body that stemmed from the life and teaching of Manes or Mani or Manichaeus, who lived in Persia in the third century A.D. But there is precedent for the wider usage now proposed: "Long before the ninth century the Greeks had adopted the epithet as a synonym for Dualist, to describe people with views like Mani's rather than followers of Mani" [1]. There were many such people at most periods. The Manichaeans—strictly so called—flourished chiefly in the fourth century: for a time they held the allegiance of the great St. Augustine, and he never entirely shook off their influence. But there is a great deal in common between their view of life and that held by the second-century Gnostics, the mediaeval Catharists and Albigensians, and the countless similar groups that emerge at intervals into the light of history, murkily obscure in their various ramifications and cross-connections. Throughout much of European history, such groups constituted a substantial religious underworld; and since the surviving record was chiefly written by their enemies, from the official Church's point of view, their story has come down to us in teasingly fragmentary form, coloured by the narrators' marked hostility.

Manichaeanism (in our broader sense of the word) has thus been present, as an alternative and rival to official Catholicism, throughout practically the whole history of the Christian West—at least, up to the time of the Reformation. With the details of its complex and obscure history, this book will not be involved[2]: our concern is with the highly characteristic view of the universe, and of the environment, which these different movements shared with remarkable unanimity. The point, at this stage, is that if we are considering various possible attitudes towards the world around us, we must bear in mind the historical importance, the plausibility, and the recurringly powerful attraction of the Manichaean attitude.

For our purposes, this can therefore be described timelessly, as though it were perfectly consistent and monolithic, which was not the case in fact: we are dealing not with the contingent events of particular ages, but rather with a pattern into which the mind of man can easily and naturally gravitate in any century, and more especially when times are difficult. It is an outlook that thrives on stress; it fits in very well with tension and grievance and fastidiousness and disappointment: it does not appeal strongly to men whose lives are fortunate and whose dispositions are easy, relaxed, and humorous. Referring to its Gnostic version, Jean Guitton[3] calls it a "widespread habit of thought, a category of the intellect, an archetype": elsewhere[4] he quotes Serge Hutin's description of it as "a religious ideology which always tends to re-appear in Europe and the Mediterranean world in times of social and political crisis." Its actual history is immensely complex, but in all its manifestations, it is recognisably the same ideology: with suitable reservations, we can usefully give it a single name and treat it as a single entity.

The thing that strikes the reader, on first encountering the ideas and writings of early Manichaeanism, is its tendency to find expression in luxuriantly intricate myth. Some people claim that in Christianity, an initially simple religion was clouded and complicated by mythological accretions: they should turn to Gnostic and Manichaean writings, and see what the full indulgence of this tendency is actually like. For most modern literary tastes, these labyrinthine writings are painfully hard going: religious and poetic in their way, they also create an impression of slight craziness, which may be partly justified. There is a sense, not to be exaggerated, in which Manichaeanism is a subject of psychiatric rather than theological interest.

De-mythologised, the Manichaean view of the universe starts off with something very simple and familiar—the sense of living in a hostile environment; the vague nostalgic feeling that we are not really at home here, but belong elsewhere; "the experience of this world as an alien place into which man has strayed and from which he may find his way back home to the other world of his origin" [5]. Stated in carefully chosen terms, this initial experience can be reconciled with something central to orthodox Christianity, the sense of exile and loss that comes from the Fall. It comes home to all of us from time to time, perhaps with great intensity; and it rings true, even at the simply biological level. This world is not a perfect home, not altogether friendly towards the naked ape: he cannot trust it completely, and at the times of additional stress mentioned by Serge Hutin, he may find it hard to control his mistrust and keep a sense of proportion. "In its most graphic form, mistrust is manifest in the paranoid vision of the world in which persons, places, and things are all invested with a malevolent power. The paranoid is thus forced to develop rituals which ward off the danger of the world or to retreat from it altogether. Expanded to metaphysical dimensions, the paranoid vision becomes gnosticism—the view that the whole world is a demon-filled prison house created by a hostile deity" [6].

And so the Manichaean outlook develops: aware of evil in himself, man projects this upon the world and even upon the Creator, and devises a theology to suit. The idea of God, and of the divine goodness, can remain; but it needs to be separated altogether from the idea of creation. Inevitably, the consequent theology is dualistic: it contrasts the good God (remote, gentle, and wholly beyond our knowing in this world) with the demiurge, the very inferior working deity who made this bad material universe. Between these two gods, the relationship is variously conceived: in one recurring version, the demiurge is equated with the stern harsh Jehovah of the Old Testament. "As the creator-god is known, obvious, and 'just', so the true God is unknown, alien, and good. He is unknown because the world can teach us nothing about him. As he had no share in creation, there is no trace in all nature from which even his existence could be suspected" [7].

Such a theology takes us far from the psalmist's joyful assertion that the heavens show forth the glory of God: far from the First Vatican Council's firm pronouncement that God is to be known "through the things that are created" [8].

In the Manichaean view, creation thus becomes an act of wickedness and cruelty: *fiat coelum, ruat iustitia*. And it is deplorable, chiefly because in the course of creation, certain sparks of real divinity—of the ultimate God, the Light, the 'cosmic Jesus'—were trapped within the corruption of this material universe. In our inward spiritual being, we *are* those sparks: our souls are actually divine, though the bodies in which they are trapped are wholly evil. Thus it is, and not on the very different lines asserted by the Christian, that we feel a sense of exile from our true home; and we can only be rescued and taken back there if God gives us knowledge (*gnosis*) of himself, and it was in order to achieve this purpose that he sent Jesus into the world. A docetist or phantasmal Jesus, of course: to the Manichaean mind, the idea of any real incarnation—especially by the ordinary road of birth—seems blasphemously obscene to the highest degree.

Man's religious task, therefore, becomes that of escaping from this evil world by cultivating a direct knowledge or *gnosis* of God. But this kind of knowledge is strictly intuitional or mystical in nature: it is quite distinct from philosophical reasoning and from Christian revelation as well, and it is profoundly incompatible with both, since both are tainted by this world.

In most of its versions, Manichaeanism is thus a theoretically ascetic religion: it calls upon men to live exactingly, despising this world and rising above it. In practice, it apparently did lead to considerable asceticism and purity of life; but this seems to have been practised chiefly by the inner ring of perfect souls, the spiritual, the élite, the adepts or *illuminati*, who in almost every Manichaean system are distinguished sharply from the common herd of imperfectly-enlightened followers. In the Middle Ages, their asceticism was sometimes extended to the point of actual suicide, usually by deliberate starvation: if Manichaean principles are to be pressed home, suicide must indeed be the ultimate act of virtue, the final liberation of the divine spark from its prison of clay. Less extreme forms of asceticism, contrasting sharply with the worldliness of the Catholic clergy, did much to win popular support for the Manichaean cults and groups of various lands and centuries. In some ways, this was always a morally upright kind of religion: it attracted people of the kind who are loosely called 'puritanical'.

But in practice—perhaps surprisingly—it also acquired a reputation of the opposite kind. Wherever Manichaeanism recurs, accusations of depravity, and of sexual depravity in particular, are almost invariably brought against it.

To some extent, these accusations can probably be discounted, as reflecting only the suspicion and hostility of Catholic contemporaries. But they certainly contain some truth, and this need not really surprise us. Manichaean beliefs, deeply cherished, can obviously generate a strong revulsion against the flesh and a consequently horrified and total kind of chastity. Phrased differently, however, or considered by a different temperament, they can lead equally well to the conclusion that since the body is Satan's realm and beyond all salvation, its activities are a matter of religious indifference. What does it matter if the corrupt body fornicates? The real self—the soul, the divine spark—remains aloof, not affected, not harmed.

Psychologically and historically too, it seems likely that Manichaean groups and communities were characteristically marked by notable asceticism and by notable permissiveness as well. Of the moral outlook of one mediaeval group, Jean Guitton says[9] that it "knows only the two extremes, the absolutely Pure and the absolutely Impure. It aims at the one and forgives the other, condemning only the middling, bourgeois way of life, which is the way of human life and of the multitudes." Other groups were positively and frankly licentious[10], seeing in promiscuity a means of setting the spirit free.

Apart from such questions of moral reputation, Manichaeanism inevitably tends to alter the content of sexuality. It involves a high assessment of love; but if taken seriously, it also involves a sharply negative attitude towards reproduction. Every birth, on the Manichaean view, is a spiritual set-back: it is a further imprisonment of God in the dirty world from which he—and our spiritual selves, his particles—must escape. It undoes the work of salvation.

In so far as it is taken seriously, a Manichaean outlook therefore tends to have three consequences for the believer's sexual life. In the first place, it tends "to devalue marriage, to deprive marital relations of any particular purpose, and to value sexual intercourse as an experience and not for the procreation that might follow" [11]. It elevates copulation into mystical communion[12], but intensely dislikes the possibility of a consequent baby. In the second place, and for that reason, it favours contraception. The Catholic attitude to this practice is well known: historically speaking, its development and formulation and the vehemence of its assertion were partly occasioned by the Church's need to oppose and resist the Manichees of different ages[13]. And in the third place, their philosophy led naturally enough to at least a relative favouring of homosexuality—a pure love, not tainted by association with birth. Here again, sweeping accusations were habitually made: as Mgr. Knox delicately observed[14], they "have left their mark upon the vocabulary of Europe". Manichaeanism was always associated strongly with the Balkans, and with Bulgaria in particular; the word *bougre*, derived from the name of that country, at one time meant simply a Dualist or Manichaean heretic[15], with no implication of homosexuality. But although these accusations were probably exaggerated, there does seem to have been a psychological and historical connection, a correlation between Manichaeanism and the kind of outlook that favours homosexuality. In particular, the social and literary movement associated with the troubadours was obscurely but definitely Manichaean in origin, and strongly homosexual in tendency and membership. It did celebrate heterosexual love, but (very pointedly) in an extremely ethereal version, idealised far above even the desire for consummation, and positively hostile to sexuality's natural follow-through in pregnancy, childbirth, and family living. It has been extremely influential in forming the erotic values, the erotic preconceptions of the modern West[16].

There is probably a close psychological link between this aspect of Manichaeanism and its recurring tendency to be anti-social. No government can really be expected to favour an ideology of which the ultimate tendency is anarchic and disruptive, hostile to family life and to any kind of structured society, hostile (in the last resort) to life itself; and if Manichees have always been subject to persecution, the motives behind this will have been social as well as theological. Already by the time of the Gnostics, they had amply displayed their characteristically contemptuous rejection of whatever would now be called 'square' and 'bourgeois', and this theme recurs down the centuries: hooked upon a vision of transcendent purity, involved also in a complex love-hate relationship with the filth of this world, the Manichee instinctively rejects and despises the arrangements and compromises of ordinary life, ordinary society, the mixed and tolerable character of the human condition in "merry middle-earth" [17]. He needs to soar or to wallow, or to soar and wallow at the same time, and he has a great contempt for ordinary unilluminated people and their ordinary way of living. Socially, morally, he can be a keen precise critic of actual evils. But his mind is essentially negative; he is always ready to criticise or to destroy, but he would betray his own principles and his own psychology if he tried seriously to create or to improve. In the last resort, he is in love with mere destruction and with death.

These are among the broad and consistent workings-out of the Manichaean mind, the Manichaean ideology. In practice, it had the most complex and erratic kind of history. In none of its manifestations, perhaps, was every one of these features fully and typically present, but they all recur with sufficient regularity to make it clear that we are dealing with something like an archetype, a coherent psychological structure, rather than with any arbitrary collection of dogmas and prejudices.

Many people were involved in it, and many of them came therefore under the full impact of the Catholic

Church's disapproval, sometimes for unexpected reasons: at one time in mediaeval France, a girl could get into some trouble with the Church for contumacious virginity[18], since in the absence of religious vows, this could indicate a Manichaean hatred of the flesh. But it would be unrealistic to suppose that all the people associated with all the versions of this ideology were in fact deeply suffused with the fully Manichaean view of life. All religious groups have fellow-travellers, uncommitted to the full doctrine or perhaps unaware of it: few present-day Anglicans, perhaps, really believe that "Works done before the grace of Christ . . . have the nature of sin"[19]. Many people must have turned to Manichaean cults quite vaguely, under the personal influence of some casual preacher; others will have been motivated by anti-Catholic and especially by anti-clerical sentiments, or will have felt a natural attraction to any kind of underground Church that opposed the establishment of the day.

But many must have joined in full understanding and agreement: the fully Manichaean outlook was certainly and powerfully present, and was preached widely and with passion, throughout much of European history. An awareness of this fact, and of what was implied, may possibly qualify our natural response to the fact of persecution. When we hear that 'heretics' have been persecuted, we are indignant, and (in the opinion of the present writer) very properly so. But we may have a vague feeling that the heretics in question were nice ordinary people, very much like the Wesleyan congregation down the road: people with their own point of view and their own manner of worshipping, but inoffensive people, no fit objects for public anger. It may help us to see things in perspective if we remember that the Manichaean heretic, at his most characteristic, was a man who hated this world, sought the disruption of society, despised marriage, saw birth as a disaster, favoured perversion, and looked upon suicide as the ultimate act of piety. He desired these views to be preached and to prevail.

Persecutions and Inquisitions are never to be justified, though they are always with us: their subject-matter tends to be political nowadays, rather than religious. But when we reflect upon what the paranoiac, despairing, and life-hating ideology of the Manichees was, we might be pardoned for thinking that if ever an idea *did* deserve to be stamped out, it was this one.

Manichaeanism, in its different Western versions, has never been one of the world's great religions: to speak crudely, it has never really succeeded. Stubborn, persistent, elusive before the Catholic persecutor, liable to break out in unexpected places like a bush-fire, it seemed to lack the positive dynamism that might have made it into something more than an opposition, an underground movement. Comparable ideas have prevailed much more successfully outside the European West: many of the great non-Christian religions look upon the world, and upon the problem of good and evil and the religious man's consequent task, in ways that come much closer to Manichaeanism than to orthodox Christianity.

It is only a partial and inadequate explanation to say that Western Manichaeanism was persecuted out of existence. There is more to it than that: Christianity, on such a reckoning, ought to have been persecuted out of existence at a very early stage. Sir Steven Runciman explained its failure[20] in terms of its inability to give men the hope that they need; and Manichaeanism is certainly an ideology of negativism and despair. But Runciman went so far as to express surprise that it should have attracted people at all.

"It may seem strange that a religion with so bizarre a theology and so much greater a concern for the welfare of the Light than for that of mankind should ever have won much popularity" [21].

This seems a curious blindness in a great scholar. Unsophisticated people have seldom been deterred by the bizarre aspects of any theology, any mythology: something of that kind might even be considered necessary, if our religion is to give any account or explanation of this very bizarre world. But the specific appeal of Manichaeanism, as a doctrine, ought to be obvious. It makes simple rough sense out of the human condition; it does justice to the mixed character of our experience in this life, to our nostalgic sense of exile and our instinctive equation of the 'spiritual' with the good; and with fair success, it attempts to by-pass the problem of evil, which must always remain a stumbling-block for the Christian.

And it does these things while relieving us of the burden of guilt: it locates the responsibility for evil elsewhere than in the human will. The whole concept of wickedness or sin plays a very small part, or none at all, in a Manichaean system: its place is taken by ignorance. Hence, living by such a system, you can combine the pleasures of high-minded religiosity with the alternative pleasures of self-indulgence or of asceticism, as the mood may take you. "At bottom," says Guitton of the Catharist religion[22], "it was wonderfully easy." Furthermore, its view of the human condition coincides exactly with the mood of grievance and self-pity to which most of us are sometimes prone. You may feel, at times, like an essentially noble and virtuous character who has been caught up into unworthy circumstances and treated very badly, and who (if people would only *understand*!) really deserves no blame at all. By Christian standards, this view of yourself will always be comic pomposity and illusion. But on a Manichaean view of the human condition, it corresponds exactly with the facts.

The thing that needs explanation is not the fact that Manichaeanism used to attract a following and enjoy a vigorous institutional life under great difficulties, but rather, the fact that it has passed into history. You will not find a Manichaean temple in present-day London, or even in New York: after so stubbornly long a persistence, all those related movements appear to have petered out, roughly around the time of the Reformation. The Manichaean psychology and the Manichaean imagination may still be with us, and all the more influentially if we fail to recognise them for what they are; but the Manichaean religion, with its long and complex history, has gone.

This is a shade surprising. How could a religious movement and outlook survive so variously and tenaciously through twelve or thirteen centuries of established Catholic opposition, as a strong and consistent and deeply influential undercurrent within the Western mind, and then just disappear, at a time when Europe was learning a new toleration for diverse cults and sects?

Perhaps the intellectual and cultural developments of the Renaissance killed it off: perhaps it was too mythological, too fanciful in its habitual mode of expression to survive into the new age.

But there is another possibility: it may simply have become superfluous. The human need that previously bred religious Manichaeanism may then have discovered another mode of fulfilment, very different in nature, much more rewarding in terms of hope, and possessing therefore a stronger historical dynamism.

Four

❀

This book is dedicated to two propositions. The first is that we live in a strongly Manichaean kind of society, though (for the most part) without being aware of the fact: the second is that this fact has great practical relevance to the environmental problems of the present day.

If we confine our attention to attitudes and activities of the explicitly 'religious' kind, the first of these propositions may initially seem rather far-fetched. Manichaeanism, considered as an institutional religion, is obviously dead: as we have observed, the sect which St. Augustine joined and subsequently left has passed into history, and with it, the passion and ferment of the Gnostics, the Albigensians and Catharists. One small Gnostic sect does survive as such, the Mandaean sect of Iraq[1]; but in general, one might be forgiven for supposing that this long chapter in the history of religion had been finally closed many years ago. That tortuously mythological way of thinking seems utterly alien to the modern mind, in its method and in its content as well. Our scientific culture talks a great deal about the visible universe, but very seldom in terms of its inherently good or evil character, and it would be startling

to hear a frankly dualistic theology proclaimed today. At a
time when it is hard enough to get men interested in a single God, we hardly expect to hear the preaching of two—
especially if the second is more or less diabolical in nature.
For some reason—it is plainly not a scientific reason—
even the religious people of today seem to be ill at ease
with the very Scriptural notion of evil spirits. Defensively,
they tend to mock at such superstitious ideas: as Screwtape observed with some complacency[2], " 'devils' are
predominantly *comic* figures in the modern imagination."

But if we turn from explicit and institutionalised religion
to the imaginative and psychological modes of experience,
we shall indeed find many converging signs that we of the
present-day West do live in a notably Manichaean society:
more precisely, that within the complex patterns of the
twentieth-century mind, there are conspicuous elements
that echo and repeat—in idioms chiefly secular—the old
pattern of the dualistic, Gnostic, and Manichaean approach to religion.

This can be stated the other way round. If Christians
still believe positively in the goodness and even the holiness of God's creation, the visible environment, they face
an urgent task of defending that paradoxical doctrine very
energetically. It is alien and uncongenial to the spirit of the
age: incessantly, it comes under a subtle kind of attack,
hardly intended on the one side, not easily recognised on
the other. The old enemy appears in disguise.

It is always rash to generalise about the spirit of an age,
the experience of a century, of a whole culture. People are
numerous and diverse: within their total experience, there
are elements that never change and elements that defy realistic generalisation. The cultural historian, concerned always to trace large consistent patterns of change, is there-

fore tempted to exaggerate the significance of his findings. Confronted by the large chaotic ragbag of historical data, he is in danger of reading into it some pattern that comes from his own preoccupations and his own subconscious mind, and of ignoring whatever fails to fit. His grand generalisations are always to be taken with a pinch of salt.

With all allowance made for this kind of scepticism, it is still very hard to study the distinctive art and literature of our time without detecting there, in dominant influence, the sentiment which gives their original impulse to all Gnostic and Manichaean systems—the feeling of alienation, the sense of a sharp and sad discontinuity between mankind and the rest of nature. Cautiously but still with a certain confidence, we can say that modern man feels himself to be estranged from this world, to be very imperfectly at home in it, alienated in a degree not suffered by previous cultures. Christianity, with its talk of original sin, always saw this life as an exile and directed men's attention towards their real home in heaven. But along with this, in a kind of balanced dialectic, there went a strong assertion of our continuity with the rest of created Nature. Man was formed from the dust of the earth, not introduced into this world from the outside, as an alien: if he was to live here as lord of creation, he was to rule as *primus inter pares*, related to the angels in one direction but to the beasts in another. He had his place in the universe, knew it, and knew that it was a crucial place. Such ideas reached their fullest expression in the mediaeval idea of the 'Great Chain of Being' that united all creation, from the highest angels to the lowest kind of unformed matter. Such a view consorts naturally with a strongly-believed theism: alongside the immense ontological gulf that separates the Creator from all his creatures, no other gulf or cleavage can seem very important.

Whatever our view of its truth, there was obvious psychological comfort in such a view of life. Mediaeval man was convinced of original sin and suffered temporal hardships far worse than ours, but his literature reflects a fundamental confidence in the universe, a sense of belonging there, qualified by belief in a further destiny but strong in the meantime: the characteristic modern feeling of alienation is completely absent from it.

In this connection, we can perhaps look upon the Darwinian revolution of the nineteenth century as a missed opportunity. It was, among other things, a re-assertion of our continuity with the animal world, and indeed with the vegetable and mineral worlds too: we were told with some vehemence that we were promoted apes in fact, whatever Disraeli might prefer or churchmen maintain. There was certainly a lesson to be learned there. If Darwin had caused us to feel, effectively, that the animals and the trees and the rocks were our close blood-relations, our alienation might have been eased. We might even have noticed, a little earlier, that there is a threat of self-destruction implied in the very idea of man conquering Nature.

But in practise, evolutionary thought—with its emphasis upon process—seems to have had the converse effect: the thing that got across was not so much our continuing unity with the beasts, but rather the fact that we have left them behind, moving on into the estranged solitude that we now find so hard to bear.

This estrangement seems to be part of the price that we necessarily pay for science and for the consequent blessings of technology. The new scientific method that came in about the time of the Renaissance depended upon detached observation: it emphasised the discontinuity between the perceiving eye and the perceived object, the Cartesian sundering of the self from the environment, and it strongly discouraged man's old sense of empathy with a world seen in anthropomorphic and animistic terms, towards which an 'I-thou' relationship might be appropriate. It never proved that Nature was a dead object in fact, devoid of all objective presences and values; but it demonstrated very clearly that by treating Nature as such a dead object—a specimen for the dissecting table, a mine to be worked, and nothing more—and by overriding all his contrary impulses, man could achieve some very spectacular results, at a price that seemed for several centuries to be low. "By reducing Nature to her mathematical elements it substituted a mechanical for a genial or animistic conception of the universe. The world was emptied, first of her indwelling spirits, then of her occult sympathies and antipathies, finally of her colours, smells, and tastes. (Kepler at the beginning of his career explained the motion of the planets by their *animae motrices*: before he died, he explained it mathematically.) The result was dualism rather than materialism. The mind, on whose ideal constructions the whole method depended, stood over against its object in ever sharper dissimilarity. Man with his new powers became rich like Midas, but all that he touched had gone dead and cold " [3].

Hence, the scientific revolution brought with it a depersonalisation and a desacralisation of Nature. "In antiquity", says Dr. Lynn White Jr.[4], "every tree, every spring, every stream, every hill had its own *genius loci*, its guardian spirit. These spirits were accessible to man, but were very unlike men; centaurs, fauns, and mermaids show their ambivalence. Before one cut down a tree, mined a mountain, or dammed a brook, it was important to placate the spirit in charge of that particular situation, and to keep it placated." Such a mentality seems infinitely remote from our own, like an echo of lost childhood, suddenly remembered in middle age but irrecoverable. "For most men in the Western world, the 'great god Pan is dead', as D. H. Lawrence declared: the woods no longer speak to us of Artemis, nor do 'the heavens declare the glory of God'. Nature does not radiate a Presence; it provides us with the raw materials to be converted into artefacts that we desire" [5].

It may be our first instinct to claim that if we have suffered a psychological loss by this change, we have also profited in terms of factual knowledge and useful power; and while 'superstition' is perhaps a question-begging term, it seems neither desirable nor possible to revive the animistic feeling for Nature in its ancient form. But if anything like the doctrine of God's immanence is true, if the Manichees are wrong in their idea of creation, it seems less obvious that we have gained in knowledge, in objectivity, by the death of Pan. It might be more precise to say that we have gained enormously in one highly specialised kind of knowledge, while losing to a comparable or greater degree elsewhere, and paying at least a heavy psychological price.

"Where is the wisdom we have lost in knowledge?
Where is the knowledge we have lost in information?" [6]

The overall profit of the transaction is disputable.

Modern man's sense of alienation is notorious. Rousseau blamed it upon the artificial life of cities: Marx blamed it upon the exploitation of the worker and the depersonalisation of his labour: both explanations seem inadequate or worse. But however it is to be understood, this sense of loneliness in a mindless and absurd universe, this sense of alienation from the environment, haunts the twentieth-century mind on strongly Gnostic and Manichaean lines, and perhaps more painfully than in the old days.

Whereas the ancient Manichees could see Nature as bad and hostile, modern man can attribute nothing but indifference to it, an awful empty neutrality that paralyses the soul. "This makes modern nihilism infinitely more radical and more desperate than Gnostic nihilism could ever be, for all its panic terror of the world and its defiant contempt of its laws. That nature does not care, one way or the other, is the true abyss" [7]. As in our personal relationships, we find indifference the worst thing of all: we experience it not as neutrality but as the extreme of hostility, and we would rather be hated than ignored. "The inscrutable power by which we are, is either for us or against us. If it is neutral, heedless of the affirmations or denials of the creatures by each other, it is against us, to be distrusted as profoundly as if it were actively inimical. For then it has cast us into being as aliens, as beings that do not fit" [8].

With proper and limited reservations, we can call this the characteristically modern view of the human predicament; and it is emphatically Manichaean in nature. We are aliens here, we do not belong: not in casual details, but essentially, we are at war with our environment. Through no fault of our own, we have been trapped into a hostile world.

In this rock-bottom sense, we can reasonably attribute a Gnostic or Manichaean character to the distinctive outlook that finds expression in the distinctive literature of the modern age; and indeed, this observation is not a new one. But it can be taken a stage further: theological dualism and the concept of a demiurge are ideas that come closer to the modern outlook than we might at first suppose.

Religion, of any kind, may be hard to put across in our times. Even so, full-blooded dogmatic atheism is probably rare. Much more widely, there prevails a kind of distantly respectful deism, with God cautiously tolerated, provided always that he keeps his distance and remains thoroughly abstract and bloodless and theoretical, not interfering too rudely in our private affairs. The sense of creation tends to be faint, the sense of God's immanent presence and action tends to be absent altogether: thus the theological problem of evil can be by-passed, at the price of a considerable attenuation in our basic religious sense.

But this is not the whole story. The old Manichees believed that our material world is made and managed not by the high and pure God, the Absolute, but by a spirit of far lower dignity, a *demiourgos* or humble worker, so far debased below divinity as to become—in some systems—almost a devil. And in an imaginatively identical way, many of these modern half-believers also have their demiurge or subsidiary working deity, distinct from the high God, much more closely involved with ourselves and our fate. They call him Evolution.

'Evolution' is of course a most useful word for scientific purposes—a shorthand term, used to cover a great many natural phenomena and processes, observed and inferred, as seen in one particular light. But where a noun exists, people often drift into the vague idea that there must be a thing, or even a Being, to correspond with it; and on these lines, there is a popular but most unscientific tendency to give evolution a capital E, and then to talk as though it were the name of a concrete entity, an actual Being of great power and dignity. At the level of conscious belief, this habit of mind would presumably be repudiated almost everywhere: at a less conscious level, it prevails very widely, and can be brought almost to the surface by careful interrogation. Somebody asserts his nominal belief that God made the world: lead him on to develop this theme, and quite often it will become apparent before long that his mind really works on rather different lines, with Evolution making this world and ourselves and now guiding us along its chosen path, while that high God remains aloof and uninvolved.

An idea originally scientific thus takes on a definitely religious and even moralistic flavour. People sometimes find it possible to ask what Evolution is doing, or what Evolution intends for our future: it is no rare thing to hear it suggested—perhaps with vehemence—that man has a moral duty to obey the will of Evolution.

In this very widespread habit of the mind, it is not fanciful to see a specifically dualistic manifestation of the generally Manichaean element in the modern outlook. It is a confused manifestation: Evolution is a sub-deity in whom hope can and must be placed, whereas the demiurge was irremediably evil, so that hope lay only in an escape from his sphere of influence. But the central idea is germinally there: the imaginative dissociation of the idea of God from the idea of immediate creation and governance, the devising of an intermediate agency.

There are two other respects in which we can attribute an implicitly Manichaean character to what may be called 'the evolutionary complex'—that forward-looking dynamism, that placing of hope in the temporal future and in the process of change, which arose in the nineteenth century and still exercises great power over the modern imagination[9]. In the first place, in so far as our minds run on evolutionary lines, we shall be treating 'goodness' as a destination towards which the universe is painfully moving, rather than as a quality inherent in all being from first to last. In effect, we shall be amending Genesis to read "God saw that it might become good": we shall be denying the robust old Aristotelian and Thomistic attribution of positive goodness to all being, merely as such. There are clear hints of this in Teilhard de Chardin's famous *Hymn to*

Matter, and indeed in much of the writing of that great Gnostic visionary. In the second place, as Chesterton once pointed out[10], popular evolutionism has "substituted the Beast for the Devil. It has made us think that our enemy is what they call our 'lower nature', which means our mere lusts and appetites, things entirely innocent in themselves. The most typical moderns have joined in this. Tennyson, for instance, spoke of moral improvement as 'moving upward, working out the brute'. But was he right? Why should we work out the brute?"

Why indeed? It is pure Manichaeanism to suppose that our corporal or animal nature is evil in itself, the thing that needs to be worked out; but this idea is fostered by the evolutionary complex, with its association of change with improvement, its insistence upon the ascent of man from something lower, something relatively contemptible. Whenever the word 'spiritual' is used as a term of simple approval or praise, this tendency becomes explicit: as a corrective, one needs to remember that according to Christian tradition, Satan himself is a most purely spiritual character.

As Belloc once observed, the body needs to be recognised and the soul kept in its place. We should not think poorly of the animals, or pride ourselves too simply upon our 'ascent' above their level. They often seem to behave much better and more reasonably than we do: they seem to retain an enviable sense of belonging in this world. On the Christian view, we have a destiny higher than theirs; but if that view is to be doubted, and in any case immediately, our 'ascent' is hardly an unqualified glory.

The secular culture of the present day thus favours a view of the universe, and of the human condition, which departs from the Christian view conspicuously; and in no random fashion of general abandonment, but in specifically dualistic and Manichaean directions. The tendency could be exaggerated: it is certainly present.

Something similar is true of the terms in which our society tends to envisage any possible remedy. For the Christian, the root of our troubles lies in sin, in the misuse of free will: the only remedy, the only hope lies in repentance and salvation by the blood of Christ. For the Manichee of old, by contrast, hope lay in *gnosis*; and while this was a religious and even a mystical concept, it has its secular counterpart today. Modern man is curiously reluctant to diagnose his troubles in terms of sin, despite the manifest wickedness that fills his newspapers: in his colloquial vocabulary, 'sin' has become a facetious synonym for fornication, and he commonly thinks of 'guilt' as an unfortunately obsessive illusion, rather than an ugly fact. With the help of a psycho-analytical priesthood, he often attempts to remedy that illusion by way of inward illumination; he aspires towards a penal system that will be primarily re-educative, cleansed of the barbaric notion of retribution; where sexual difficulties and disasters exist, he puts extraordinary faith in sexual education, as though the well-informed were commonly the well-behaved. In knowledge, and particularly in self-knowledge, he sees the road to goodness.

From this tendency to diagnose our troubles in terms of ignorance, two manifest social consequences follow. In the first place, modern man puts a quite unrealistic amount of faith in the process of education, dedicating huge resources to the highly questionable proposition that it is an automatically good thing for anybody to be in any kind of classroom or lecture-room at any time for any kind of purpose, and to the further proposition that mere research—

the acquisition of further knowledge—is a prime and most urgent task.

> "Life is a vale, its paths are dark and rough
> Only because we do not know enough:
> When Science has discovered something more
> We shall be happier than we were before" [11].

The stresses generated by this quasi-Gnostic illusion are starting to trouble the university scene: it might be no bad thing if research slowed down or stopped for a while, thus allowing poor bewildered breathless humanity to catch up and digest some of its recently-accumulated knowledge.

In the second place, modern man puts a similarly exaggerated kind of faith in the intelligentsia, the caste of adepts or *illuminati* which nearly always separates itself out in any Manichaean group or society, claiming a priestly position of insight and leadership, far above the common herd. This faith is sometimes rationalised as a belief in the strictly intellectual process, in reason and clear thinking. It can have that character in fact: given the general bewilderment of humanity, the trained minds of a minority can indeed provide us with needed leadership and with assistance towards a closer grip on reality. But it is unrealistic—and it is becoming more and more obviously unrealistic—to associate the intelligentsia with the intellect. The dominant *illuminati* and the rigorously logical reasoners are no longer always—or even commonly—the same people: a man can preach a passionately visceral and anti-rational doctrine without in the least diminishing his status among the intellectuals. Increasingly, this priesthood is concerned with *gnosis* in something like the old sense: so far as the *avant-garde* intelligentsia are concerned, there is much truth in "the McLuhanite theory that the art of communication is passing from the straight, hard, linear man of the Gutenberg Galaxy into the noisy psychedelic womb of sound, sensation, sniff, touch, and hash" [12].

Notoriously, this change is one of the most conspicuous cultural phenomena of the day; and it leads to a cleavage, a polarisation in society, with feelings running high on either side. Whereas we once distinguished the educated classes from the ignorant, or the rich from the poor, we are now more intensely aware of another distinction. On the one side we see the swinging hipster world of the _illuminati_, anarchic, dionysiac, aware, seeking _gnosis_ not through education and reason but rather through drugs and pop and the drug-use of sexuality; and on the other we see the square world of bourgeois living and linear thought.

To read about the old-time Gnostics and Manichees is to be reminded incessantly, and very closely indeed, of this present-day polarisation, this contention that is so often over-simplified into a mere Oedipal conflict between the generations. Very widely, we can agree, Christianity has been abandoned; and in 'square' society, the worship of Mammon has tended to take its place. But Mammon makes a very unsatisfactory god; and what we now see, not only among the long-haired young, is an impassioned revival of the old Gnostic dream with all its natural concomitants—a contempt for society, for law and order, for quotidian experience, and a seeking instead of rebellious transcendence, of 'authentic existence', of shattering sensation, of escape.

It is essentially a hatred of this world as given. In their use of the word _cosmos_, the Stoics implied a feeling of praise and admiration for the beauty and order of this world[13]; then the Gnostics took that word over and reversed its value, turning it into a term of contempt. Their present-day counterparts go in for similar reversals, crying positively for madness and upheaval and destruction: they are hostile to life, and especially to the given and limited quality that ordinary life possesses, and they rationalise this hostility by directing it—nominally—at particular institutions and happenings and structures in society. But all this is an excuse: alleviate one grievance, and you only put them to the trouble of finding another. Their real need is to denounce the universe and drop out of it.

There are a host of senses in which we can say that the characteristic posture of modern man is one of distrust and hostility towards this world, towards Nature, towards human experience in its given and limited character.

This is notably true in the matter of sex. Protesting too loudly to carry much conviction, our world claims to have shaken off the old fears and taboos and to be now recovering an easy, frank, natural acceptance of sexuality as a happy fact of daily life. This is one of the great and comical hypocrisies of the day: it would not be too much of an exaggeration to say that our society is actually engaged in a headlong panic-stricken flight from what sexuality is. It is as though we hated and feared the goddess Venus—and perhaps understandably, since she does have her terrors—and were trying rather desperately to reassure ourselves by mutual hyponosis and mutual deception. We try to hide from what she is: in a thousand ways, we display our almost frantic preference for altered sex, for doctored sex, for imitation sex, for dream-and-fantasy sex. Never was there such a market for voyeuristic and masturbatory aids to illusion in this matter: every day, we read of some new manifestation of our culture's obsessive flight from sex.

At another and possibly a higher level, our society has a

marked tendency to discount and even to despise the biological function of sexuality, valuing it instead as an experience and a road to *gnosis*, to illumination and the transcendence of self. "Human intelligence and industry," says Jean Guitton[14], "have at all times been engaged in dissociating sex from procreation and even from love. There is concealed beneath all these attempts a metaphysical notion from which they draw their secret energy and sustenance. It is the notion that God the Creator did not stoop to create matter or involve himself in it. He was content to cast a few pure sparks into this clay."

It seems clear that present-day society is pervaded by a positive cult of sterility, a preference for contraception and for a sexuality seen in non-biological, non-reproductive terms. The population question, as one element in the environmental and ecological crisis of the present time, will be discussed in a later chapter: the present point is that the existence and urgency of this question appears to be almost welcomed in many quarters, as providing so splendid a rationalisation and excuse for essentially Manichaean attitudes towards sex.

There is a fear of life, a hatred of birth. Venus is a fertility-goddess, and we are terrified of what she is in herself, quite apart from what too much fertility might do to our families or our world. If the protestations of this liberated and permissive society were to be taken at their face value, our outspoken novels would be charged with a spirit of happy pagan relish for what Venus is, a joyous celebration of reproductive carnality. In fact, as every critic knows, this is seldom the case. In Henry Miller's *Tropic of Cancer*, sexuality is a matter of loveless despair; in Norman Mailer's *An American Dream*, it works out consistently as a preference for sodomy (a death-thing) over procreation (a life-thing). These are rightly seen as seminal and formative novels, voicing the outlook of this age, typical of many: in the characteristic utterances of our society, sex becomes either a triviality—personal hygiene, private fun —or else, and more often, a kind of nightmare. The divinity of Venus is quite forgotten: she too has been desacralised.

Perhaps we found it hard to forgive her for representing so obstinately powerful a natural force, so resistant to our domination. We conquered electricity, we conquered the atom, we raped the moon, but Venus held out. No wonder men love the Pill: it is the magic bullet that will at last bring down the hated enemy and bend her to our will.

It was suggested above that the Manichaean tendencies in our society wear secular garments, not appearing in frankly theological and ecclesiastical forms. Even so, the Churches have not been immune from their infection.

During these last few years, the Christian world has plunged into a new flux and ferment, doubtlessly exaggerated by the news-media, but undeniably genuine. Old certainties have been questioned and widely cast aside, the old authority of Pope and Council and hierarchy and scripture and tradition has been radically re-assessed. From the new situation so created—a chaotic situation, by older standards—various coherent patterns are starting to emerge, constituting perhaps a new Christianity, which some will welcome and others will deplore; and in a great many respects, it looks like a Christianity modified in a definitely Manichaean and especially in a Gnostic direction.

This may seem an eccentric suggestion: nominally at least, many of the characteristic theological movements of the time are oriented towards a greater involvement in this world. But such movements tend to be eschatological and millenniarist in their mood: so far from emphasising the ontological goodness of this world in its present state—and our personal duty of achieving a corresponding goodness—they seek rather an upheaval and a transformation to be achieved collectively. Commonly in semi-political terms, they emphasise the present badness of our life, our society, while playing down the idea of personal guilt: they are often associated closely with the cult of grievance.

To read of the ideas and practices that characterised religious Manichaeanism in its various historical versions is to be reminded sharply of various well-publicised trends in present-day Christianity. One reads, for example, of a habitual impatience with hierarchy and the institutional Church, with a recurring wisecrack[15] about how Rome (*Roma*) inverts the very name of God and Love (*Amor*); a strong emphasis upon scripture (rather selectively read) and upon brotherhood, as against the Real Presence in the Eucharist; a relative toleration of sexual licence, and in particular of homosexual and contraceptive practices; a socially disruptive anarchism, contemptuous towards bourgeois values; a strong verbal emphasis upon poverty and peace, and upon 'love' in slightly questionable senses of that complicated word; a sharp dislike of what Protestants used to call 'Mariolatry'; a rejection of grand church buildings and of lofty ritual; a systematic playing-down of the concept of sin or guilt, and a consequent denial of Hell; and a somewhat Pharisaical tendency to claim a monopoly of the Holy Spirit and of virtue. Underlying these things, one finds an impatience with the principle of Incarnation: where the central doctrine is not flatly rejected, one finds a rejection of its ecclesiastical, eucharistic, and Mariological implications. Manichees and sub-Manichees have always had their teeth set on edge by the idea that God might really involve himself and really be present in this imperfect world and especially in this plainly imperfect Church. One can hardly blame them: it is a perennially difficult idea.

All this is familiar ground to present-day Catholics, and to others as well: any account of old-style Manichaeanism makes highly topical reading for the student of today's religious trends. Perhaps the most significant thing here is the extraordinary emphasis placed nowadays upon the concept of *gnosis*, in something like the ancient understanding of that word: the new sort of theological writing is characteristically packed to bursting-point with its various near-synonyms or near-translations—with 'insight', with 'awareness', with 'meaning', with 'experience', given always the central dignity appropriate to an absolute value. Increasingly, the Christian religion is coming to be seen as an illuminism, a transcendence, an escape from the burden of self which (according to older and more orthodox writers) needs to be conquered rather than evaded.

They claim that the older theology lacks relevance: as indeed it does, if the human problem is to be initially seen in Gnostic terms.

Even among Christians, the Manichaean tendency is manifest: the attribution of goodness to this world and to our quotidian experience within it, so that grace needs only to perfect Nature and not to replace it, is a doctrine which needs defending. In sacred and secular matters alike, it shows itself alien to the spirit of this age.

Five

❄

Outstandingly, however, and on a far larger scale, the old Manichaean impulse finds present-day expression in something not mentioned in the last chapter—in the huge blind assault upon Nature that technology becomes when it ceases to be governed by real human need and takes on the character of a self-justifying activity. Increasingly since the middle of the last century, this assault has been the chief and characteristic business of our society: for mere conquest's sake, we are collectively engaged in fighting the environment, and to our many successes in this conflict, we attach optimistic labels like 'progress'.

It now turns out that this enterprise leads to an environmental crisis that threatens our whole future. This should not surprise us: it is in accordance with precedent. In rejecting the cosmos, in setting up as Nature's adversary, Manichaean man always rejected the basis of his own earthly life: the logical conclusion of his outlook was always suicide.

In this perspective, it ceases to be remarkable that religious and institutional Manichaeanism should have disappeared from the European scene several centuries ago. It became superfluous.

Life in this world was always difficult and painful. But with the Renaissance, with the first beginnings of modern science and technology, it began to be possible for man to *do* something about his unsatisfactory condition, and with increasing hope of success. In previous centuries he could only endure, devising theologies to explain his torment and (to the best of his ability) justifying the ways of God to man. But now a new road was open. The starting-point of Manichaeanism would remain—that old recurring sense that Nature is hostile and alien, that we deserve a better world. But this feeling could now become the starting-point of a programme of action, rather than of a theology: ceasing to be the trade-mark of a malign demiurge, Nature's hostility could become a challenge instead, a challenge that we could accept with increasing confidence. We were no longer helpless: we could fight that demiurge on his own ground. Man's conquest of Nature could begin, initially in order to ease the real pains of our condition. But once it had fairly begun, the old Manichaean motivation would cause it to continue for its own sake, as a punitive campaign and an act of corporate self-assertion on the part of the human race, far beyond any relevance to our real troubles and our real needs.

Modern technology and the old Manichaean religion might seem, at first sight, to be as dissimilar as two fields of human attention could possibly be. But they have roots and motivations in common: in a real sense, they are alternative responses—of fight and flight respectively—to one single element in experience, the intractability, the apparent hostility of Nature. Between those ancient cults and our present technological practices, there is a kind of continuity: the cults became superfluous and faded from the scene as the practices gained in scope and confidence. And now that the practices have begun to prove less innocuous than we supposed, the mentality that lies behind both needs reappraisal.

The question has a practical urgency that may well overshadow its theoretical and religious urgency. But paradoxically, we may need to consider the theoretical and religious questions first: sound action can only be based on sound belief.

Since the environmental crisis first became a matter of public concern, it has become a commonplace to accuse technological man of gross aggressiveness towards Nature, and to assert that a change of practice is necessary and a change of heart as well. About the required change of practice, there is a fair measure of short-term agreement. Man's lust for random domination has to be brought under control: large new technological developments have to be carefully and suspiciously scrutinised, and can no longer be justified simply by the immediate benefits that they confer: resources have to be conserved: the rising tide of environmental pollution must be halted and reversed. Most writers conclude the argument, and many begin it, with emphatic pleadings for population control.

On these lines, there are many calls and pressures for legislation and for other kinds of positive action, at the local, national, and international levels. But in the last resort, human behaviour is governed by ideas and attitudes and beliefs rather than by legislation; and there is general agreement that humanity will not cope with the environmental crisis, and may not even survive it, unless we achieve an extensive and effective change of heart and outlook.

But what *kind* of change? In what sense, in what direction does our present outlook need to be modified? Of what heresy do we need to repent? And how can we be sure that it *is* a heresy, an illusion or fallacy, and not merely a legitimate point of view?

About these more fundamental questions, there is little agreement at present, as might be expected in a society that lacks a common faith; and there is practically no recognition of the Manichaean impulse that lies behind blind technomania. In so far as these questions are canvassed at all, the boot tends to be on the other foot. Where the ultimately religious nature of the environmental crisis is recognised, there is a strong tendency to blame Christianity for it.

On the face of it, this seems far-fetched: the modern world hardly seems to be governed and led—for good or for ill—by any exaggerated fidelity to the teachings of the Bible and of Christ. But there is a vocal and influential school of thought which detects in the whole Judaeo-Christian tradition a chronic tendency to over-value humanity and to under-value the rest of Nature, so that people reared in that tradition tend instinctively towards a domineering and ultimately destructive attitude towards their environment. On this view, Christianity itself—and presumably Judaism as well—becomes the heresy of which we need to repent; at the very least, it must be radically modified, chiefly by the cultivation of a greater tribal humility on the part of man, and a natural or cosmic piety of the sort that has hitherto been associated with paganism and with some Eastern religions rather than with Christianity.

So the argument runs: soundly as regards its conclusion, very questionably as regards its blaming of Christianity. But many writers have seen the question sweepingly, in just those terms. Aldous Huxley, for one, was very emphatic about it[1]: "The vulgar boast of the modern technologist that man has conquered Nature has roots in the Western religious tradition, which affirms that God installed man as the boss, to whom Nature was to bring tribute. The Greeks knew better than the Jews or Christians. They knew that *hubris* towards Nature was as much of a sin as *hubris* towards fellow-men. Xerxes is punished, not only for having attacked the Greeks, but also for having outraged Nature in the affair of bridging the Hellespont. But for an ethical system that includes animate and inanimate Nature as well as man, one must go to Chinese Taoism . . ."

More recently, similar things have been said by many of those who have concerned themselves with the environmental problem. Christianity has become something of a scapegoat. "Our science and technology", says Dr. Lynn White Jr.[2], "have grown out of Christian attitudes towards man's relation to Nature, which are almost universally held not only by Christians and neo-Christians but also by those who fondly regard themselves as post-Christians. Despite Copernicus, all the cosmos rotates around our little globe. Despite Darwin, we are *not*, in our hearts, part of the natural process. We are superior to Nature, contemptuous of it, willing to use it for our slightest whim." "Western man," says Dr. René Dubos[3], "tends to consider himself apart from and above the rest of creation. He has accepted to the letter the Biblical teaching that man was given by God 'dominion over the fish of the sea, and over the fowl of the air, and over the cattle, and over all the earth' (Genesis 1:26)." "Perhaps . . . we ought to study Asian attitudes to Nature much more closely," suggests Dr. Hugh Montefiore[4], "for often-times they were less aggressive regarding 'the lower creation' than those which derive from the Judaeo-Christian tradition."

In many quarters, this kind of accusation against Christianity has become a commonplace: it reflects, among other things, the present-day tendency of Christendom and the West to display a certain apologetic defensiveness in many different matters. Allowing for that, the situation is an entertaining one to the connoisseur of controversial gymnastics. If Christianity is to take the blame for the destructive excesses of modern technomania, it must also deserve whatever credit is due to the earlier and the more beneficent achievements of a scientific and technological culture. But this credit was never given: until recently, it was the fashion to sneer loftily at the Christians —and at the Catholics in particular—for their obscurantism in connection with science, their backwardness in connection with technology and industrial development, their lack of interest in man's conquest of Nature. There was supposed to be an irreducible conflict between science and religion: those who saw new hope, new happiness for mankind in the conquest of Nature would commonly look upon the Church as their chief enemy. Christianity was the opium of the people, offering fantasies of pie-in-the-sky and thus distracting men from the immediate challenge and task of building a technological New Jerusalem here upon earth: it fostered gloom and guilt and defeatism and despair, a low vision of man's possibilities, an acquiescence in suffering that might easily be overcome. So the accusation ran; and plausibly enough, the forward-looking men of the new age could say that the priest-ridden countries were the backward ones, sunk in peasant ignorance, closer to brutish paganism than to the brave new world which man's conquest of Nature was bringing to birth.

Any stigma, notoriously, will do to beat a dogma: the Christian controversialist is well accustomed to the experience of being shot at from both sides, of being told that his religion is too hard and too soft, too logical and too sentimental, too optimistic about the human condition and too pessimistic about it as well. And so, when his faith is accused of fostering aggressive technomania, he will be disposed to grin rather than to argue. Only yesterday, it was being accused of the opposite fault. How (he will wonder) would H. G. Wells have responded to the idea that there might be a causal connection between Christian belief and man's scientific conquest of Nature?

The objectors have a certain case. In the seamless web of traditional Christianity, a definite 'theology of the environment' was always implied. But it needed to be developed and rendered explicit and then preached and enacted; and in this respect, the Churches cannot be held wholly innocent of a certain lethargy, a certain failure to look ahead. Our present troubles might have been foreseen. But in the suggestion that a theology of the environment might be possible and desirable, most good Christians in the past would probably have suspected mere paradox, or perhaps a threat of pantheism, or (at the best) a straining of language and a distraction from the more serious business of religious thinking.

Within limits, such responses would have been reasonable enough. Christianity was always an other-worldly religion, centred upon a transcendent God, and upon man's task of loving and serving him in this world so as to find and enjoy him in the next. In a secondary way, it also involved the love of one's neighbour, an energetic commitment to charity and peace and happiness among men in this life. But this was the whole story: all duty, all moral-

ity (if really enjoined upon the Christian) was reducible
to one or to both of those two precepts. The precise relationship between the two might be disputed: just lately, in
the spirit of Abou ben Adhem, certain theologians have
been stressing the second at the expense of the first, as
though God were chiefly or only to be encountered in the
love and service of our neighbour. That argument continues.

But there were only those two precepts; and if it had
been suggested that the Christian profession might also
impose upon the faithful a duty towards the world as such,
the visible environment, most people would have been
sceptical until recently. 'The world' only seemed to come
into the Christian picture in two rather negative ways. It
was, of course, the morally neutral background to all our
activities, providing therefore the raw material for all our
virtues and all our vices; and in a specialised sense of the
word, it was also seen in a sharply critical light, as a temptation and snare for the spiritually-minded man, an enemy,
aptly bracketed with the flesh and the devil.

The habitual thinking of many Christians ran rather on
these lines, giving some limited excuse to those who want
to blame Christianity for modern man's arrogant handling
of Nature. The question is theologically interesting, since
it provides a simple text-book example of what Newman
had in mind when he spoke of the 'development' of doctrine. In principle a duty towards the environment was always implied in Christianity, but it is only now becoming
explicit. This does not involve any addition of new doctrines or new duties: the old twofold precept of charity remains and is sufficient. But we see new implications in it.
The love of God entails a certain respect or awe before the
work of his hands, the Creation which he loves and which
partakes (in its degree) of his own goodness; and in the

same way, the love of one's neighbour entails a careful cherishing of the environment upon which he also depends, and will continue to depend in future generations.

We are beginning to see this now: we need to see it more clearly: we ought to have seen it before. We always knew about that twofold precept of charity, but in neglecting to work out its full implications soon enough, we left our defences against Manichaeanism undesirably weak. That subtle enemy infiltrated, helped along by ambiguities in the language of devotion and even of Scripture. We speak of 'the world, the flesh, and the Devil', and there are still some of us who equate that 'world' with the world that God made and loved and died for. It is an elementary mistake: St Francis was the least 'worldly' of men, but his *Canticle of the Sun* is suffused with the love of God's visible creation. We should not confuse these two senses of the word, or suppose (as many do) that when St Paul speaks adversely of 'the flesh', he is referring to sexuality and declaring it evil. Such mistakes have been made too often: despite creation, despite incarnation, despite sacrament, Christians have often tended to be shaky about the goodness of Nature.

But if, on these lines, they have failed to take a sufficiently strong stand against man's arrogant misuse of the world, this has not been because of their Christianity but because of their failure in Christianity, their vague semi-heretical leanings in a Manichaean direction. The remedy lies in a fuller working-out and a more vigorous application of what their religion always contained; and this will exclude every kind of arrogance or contempt towards the visible creation. It will not down-grade man. Christian theology always gave him a special place in the world, a place of authority, of qualified dominion and mastery. But authority, properly exercised, is an exacting thing, quite incompatible with casualness and contempt and exploitation. And in any case, the world remained God's property. Man had the privileges of a life tenant and the responsibilities of a steward, but he was never a freeholder, and he was answerable always to the Landlord. "Man is placed in the world by God to be its lord. He is meant to have dominion over it and to use it . . . but only for God's sake, only like Adam in Paradise, cultivating it for the Lord. As soon as he begins to use it selfishly, and reaches out to take the fruit which is forbidden by the Lord, instantly the ecological balance is upset and Nature begins to groan" [5].

The idea of man's dominion over Nature is certainly present in Christianity. But it does not exist there in isolation: it is modified and controlled by other ideas—the overlordship of God, his immanence in creation (which does not exclude his transcendence of it), the goodness of all being, the wickedness of all arrogance and self-will, our perennial need for restraint and humility and obedience. 'Man's conquest of Nature' is not—for good or for ill—a concept that arises directly and naturally from the Judaeo-Christian view of the world. On the contrary: it embodies, very precisely, the Manichaean view of the world that was always Christianity's chief enemy.

If this were not the case, science and technology—in our modern understanding of those words—would have had a different and perhaps a longer history: they would have stemmed directly from the Christian culture, and psychologically speaking, they would have always been at peace with it.

This is hardly what happened in fact. The scientific and technological culture of today certainly originated in the Christian West, in Europe, though Arabic influence was important; and though it now governs life in every conti-

nent and under all religions and ideologies, it does so by
inviting other peoples to think and behave on lines that are
European by origin.

It does not follow, however, that in any real sense we
ought to thank Christianity for the blessings, and blame it
for the dangerous excesses, of technology. Between these
two cultures, the Christian and the technological, there
was some continuity of intellectual method but a very
sharp discontinuity of value and purpose. The transition
was revolutionary, and was felt on either side to have that
character: it was not by any means a matter of smooth
linear development, of old principles carried one stage further. Our scientific and technological culture was rooted in
the new humanism, the new secularism, the repudiation of
Christian values that began cautiously at the time of the
Renaissance and has been gathering momentum ever
since; it involved a new isolation and enthronement of
man, a break-up of the old 'chain of being', a new pride, a
new hope of conquest. Its prophets were men like Bacon
and Marlowe: the whole story, including its ending, is
summed up in Marlowe's *Faustus*.

No reasonable person considers science and technology
to be inherently evil, inherently anti-Christian. None the
less, the story of their early development is closely associated with the story of a more or less violent departure from
Christianity: a departure, moreover, in a direction closely
analogous to the direction previously taken by religious
Manichaeanism. It sundered man from his environment
and placed the two in opposition: it desacralised the world
and emphasised the remoteness of God: by making the
modification of Nature by technique into the principal
business of man, it implied (at the least) an immense
qualification of her inherent goodness.

Between this new culture and Christianity, there was an

immediate though confused recognition of mutual hostility. Those somewhat dated controversialists, of Wells's tribe, had a valid point. Deeply religious societies have tended, during these last four hundred years, to be technologically backward: science and religion have tended to bristle at one another. Questions of value, rather than questions of fact, were at stake. Science and religion were not really in dogmatic contradiction, though there were intellectual difficulties and confusions on both sides: it is more to the point to say that they were in competition. Psychologically and imaginatively, if not logically, the scientific and technological complex seems to function as an alternative or even a rival to Christianity: it is something like a religion, an objective towards which men can direct their faith, their hope, their dedication.

It is, perhaps, the established religion of our time: there may be underground doubts and infidelities, as is usual with established religions, but when men speak in their public and official capacities, it is in those terms that they tend most naturally to see their central collective preoccupation, the chief business of life. It would not be too fanciful to say that for some time past, most of us have worshipped an Unholy Trinity—Science in the first place; then, Science's child, Technology; and then, the Standard of Living that proceeds from both and has descended upon our world so abundantly.

The blessings that we have thus received have been enormous; and if the cynic were to argue that this Trinity makes better sense than the one proposed by Christianity —and functions more effectively too, delivering the goods more certainly and on easier terms—he would have had a strong *prima facie* case until recently.

Now, however, there appears to be a certain change of heart, a certain weakening in faith. If people are becoming very reasonably nervous about the environmental hell that blind technomania threatens to inflict upon them, they are also starting to get bored with the heaven which—at the best—it offers.

We do not know how far this combination of fear and boredom will take us. Quite conceivably, we may shortly find ourselves living in a post-scientific, post-technological world. This would not necessarily be agreeable: we are unlikely to find ourselves dancing round the maypole and quaffing ale in a rustic paradise. If the idols of scientific and technological progress start to topple, other and more unpleasant deities may well take their place.

But blind technomania is ceasing to be plausible as an absolute, a thing to be fostered and served uncritically. It needs reappraisal and control: the environmental crisis brings this fact home to us very sharply. As Jacques Ellul has pointed out[6], technology develops causally, not teleologically: the lines of its development are not necessarily harmful to human well-being, so much as irrelevant to it. We could do with a better deity: this one is totally indifferent to ourselves and our fate.

It may indeed be on the decline. For one thing, it depends upon science; and the whole habit of scientific thought and action depends in turn upon certain assumptions—concerning the order and uniformity of the universe, the validity of reasoning and of inductive logic in particular, and the intelligibility of phenomena—such as have not been obvious to all men at all times, and are by no means certain to continue as part of our own mental furniture. These assumptions are not in themselves scientific: they have, rather, a religious character, and their possibilities first began to develop in a place and time marked by a sudden deflection of the scholastic mind from its original theological object. Within the scientific and technological complex, they constitute the one element that really is Christian in origin and character. The theologian and the scientist agree that the cosmos makes sense: the old Gnostic and the modern existentialist agree that the cosmos does not make sense.

Whether 'science' of the modern sort could ever, conceivably, have arisen *except* in a post-scholastic age would make an interesting subject for speculative enquiry: a more pressing question concerns the continued viability of science and a science-based culture in a world increasingly unsure about those assumptions or any other, a world that shows diminishing concern for intellectual rigour and an increasing preference for intuition and illuminism, a world that seems less and less concerned to pay even lip-service to such concepts as reason, order, and objective meaning.

Meanwhile, the environmental crisis calls us to a change of heart, a repudiation of whatever way of thinking may have caused technology to get so destructively out of control.

The ultimately decisive factor here will be our attitude to religion, and to the doctrine of this world's goodness in particular. In so far as technological activity is motivated by something like the love of God and the love of one's neighbour, and limited by a lively respect for the goodness of all created being, it is likely to be beneficial or at least fairly harmless. But in so far as it is motivated by anything like a simple desire to conquer Nature for conquest's sake and for the glorification of Man, it will be a Manichaean thing, and sooner or later it will implement the death-wish that resides in all Manichaeanism. The environmental crisis brings this fact home to us, reminding us that we should have treated this excellent world more lovingly. But technology gave us new powers at a time when the Christian influence was declining; and we therefore used those new powers, not only to ease our real hardships, but also to implement that subliminal hostility towards the world which—in earlier ages—could only find expression in anti-Christian theologies and cults.

This would be a grossly exaggerated view, a caricature, if the vast technological effort of our society did in fact work teleologically, and was wholly—or even chiefly—ordered on a realistic basis towards human well-being and human happiness. No Manichaeanism need be implied in the simple desire to be comfortable and to enjoy life, or in such modification of the environment as these innocent purposes may dictate: technological in their degree, the bees and the beavers work on these lines, and nobody finds them alienated from their world. But we cannot seriously see our present activities in that kind of light. If we detach ourselves mentally from the complex routine of present-day life, and stand back, and gaze critically upon the things currently being done by technomaniac man, it becomes obvious that he is driven by motivations only partially and accidentally related to any realistic idea of his own well-being, his own happiness. He has a lofty purpose half-consciously in mind, distinct from the Epicurean pursuit of happiness, distinct also from the Christian service of God; he is engaged—for its own sake—in the conquest of Nature, and like any good soldier, he ignores the hardships that this arduous campaign inflicts upon him.

They are hardships indeed; and in a shame-faced, half-jocular way, most of us will admit the fact—guiltily, because we will thus imply a critical attitude towards the established religion. Our official line is still one of confident optimism: technomaniac man is supposed to be enjoying himself thoroughly, finding great exhilaration and fulfilment in the campaign, fortunate to be living among the fantastic and exhausting complexities of an advanced technological society. In fact, we get by: most of us adapt to such a society fairly well in a surface way, and feel disoriented and angry when it lets us down—when the electricity fails, throwing us back on candles, or when the car breaks down, throwing us back on feet. But this proves very little. Man is an adaptable animal: he becomes accustomed to familiar circumstances, and then undergoes stress if these are changed suddenly. Prisoners can feel unhappy, for a time, when let out of jail.

Secretly, we all know this. If we were called upon to show that people in technologically advanced societies are consistently happier or wiser or better than people in technologically simple societies, we would hardly know where to start: the thesis is so wildly implausible that it refutes itself before the argument begins. In practice, any attempt to argue a case of that kind would drive us back to concentrate upon the one advanced technology that really is beneficial beyond all question—the technology of medicine and of public health. It would be a genuine evil, a genuine loss and a great one, if we had to revert to a life without anaesthetics and antibiotics and aseptic surgery and indoor sanitation and running water and cheap soap. But the argument starts to lose force as soon as we try to take it beyond that very important but limited field; and we certainly cannot make any similar assertion about a life without colour television, nuclear bombs, computers, superhighways, and moon-shots. All the evidence suggests that apart from the single question of medicine, we would be much happier in a much simpler kind of society, technological up to a point but cautiously, resolute in the subordination of technical means to real human ends.

Wistfully and perhaps with little hope, one can dream of life in such a society. Already, most of us seek something like it when the coming of holiday-time allows us to forget the furious endeavours and concentrate upon simple happiness instead. But apart from these brief periods of escape, we are riding the technomaniac tiger, and it is not easy to see how we can dismount safely.

At least we can make a start on the necessary change of heart, which can now be defined with some precision: we can repent of Manichaeanism in all its versions. It was always rash, on our part, to declare unrestricted war upon Nature. The environmental crisis suggests that she may hit back; and she is a good deal stronger than us, and has no moral scruples whatever about genocide. We may have to make our peace with this formidable adversary, or else die.

At this present time we are at war with her, and on classically Manichaean lines, though this aspect of the twentieth-century outlook and way of life is seldom given its proper name. It is a rare thing to find it stated explicitly that the phenomenal universe is actually evil, or under the domination of some evil power. In the course of an eloquent defence of technomania[7], Dr. Edmund Leach comes fairly close to such an assertion: "All of us need to understand that God, or Nature, or Chance, or Evolution, or the Course of History, or whatever you like to call it, cannot be trusted any more. We simply must take charge of our own fate." But this is an unusually frank statement: for the most part, the untrustworthy, hostile, and evil character of the universe, and our consequent task of beating it down and subjecting it to our will, are implied and enacted rather than proclaimed. We seldom declare it bad; but we very seldom treat it with the restraint and respect that would come naturally if we really saw goodness and holiness in it.

The thing needed is a revived sense of that goodness

and holiness. As long as we think negatively, concentrating upon the evils of technomania, we shall be in danger of abandoning one form of Manichaeanism for another; and this danger is relevant to the great cultural divide that was mentioned in the last chapter. One might say that modern society is torn between Apollonian Manichaeanism and Dionysiac Gnosticism: between those who respond to Nature's manifest evil by fighting it, by establishing a technological domination over it, and those who respond by dropping out and tuning in ecstatically to some private wave-length of *gnosis*. The forcefully aggressive father and the limp long-haired son contend rather furiously, but they are united in ignoring the Christian, whose small voice tries to intrude with the suggestion that Nature may not be so very bad after all. Fight and flight are not the only possibilities.

In that conflict between two essentially Manichaean cultures, the Christian can hardly be neutral. The Dionysiac son, with his drugs and his death-wish, can only succeed in poisoning himself: the Apollonian father, efficient in his great plans of conquest, may quite possibly kill us all. But they are both wrong: this delicate creation deserves a response more positive, more respectful, more loving. It is indeed delicate, in the sense of being (for our purposes) extremely fragile: we are discovering this fact at last. But it is delicate in another sense too: it is a rich and rare thing, a delicacy, something to be appreciated. Our first response to it might well be gratitude; and if we are to repent of Manichaeanism, we might do so—in the first instance—because it is the most ungrateful heresy of them all.

Six

✳

"The great vice of Americans," said W. H. Auden[1], "is not materialism but a lack of respect for matter."

The vice in question is not confined to Americans. All over the world, wherever the empire of *homo techno-scientificus* extends, an ecological and environmental crisis comes into being, most acutely where that empire is most keenly served; and of this crisis, a fundamentally Manichaean contempt for matter is—if not the sufficient cause —at least the necessary condition. A society in which Nature was deeply and genuinely respected—whether on Christian or pagan lines—would hardly desire to indulge in the activities that now cause such varied and frightening kinds of trouble.

It might be our first instinct to respond to this situation pragmatically: if 'a theology of the environment' is proposed, we might take a chiefly practical kind of interest in the idea, hoping to find in it some way out of our terribly concrete difficulties. In its way, this would be a very reasonable response. Against the Manichaeanism of the day, we do have an urgent practical need to re-discover, re-assert, and enact more fully our old lost awareness that

God's delicate creation is a good and holy thing, a work and presence of divinity, not dead and empty of all objective values, not by any means evil, not an enemy. Fully recovered and deeply felt, this awareness would lead almost automatically to a radically different handling of Nature, on lines more symbiotic and less exploitative, less appropriate to an enemy and more appropriate to a mother: to adapt a phrase from Bertrand Russell, it would bring us back to a needed sense and practice of 'cosmic piety'.

For reasons entirely practical and of this world, we urgently need such a reformation: it seems quite likely to be a condition of our survival, or at least of our continued well-being. It will plainly be hard to achieve. But quite possibly, our race will only have a tolerable future over the next half-century or so if we do achieve it—*where* we do achieve it, *in so far as* we do achieve it. The kind of society that is likely to survive and prosper is the kind of society in which men would never dream—individually or collectively—of treating Nature in the disrespectfully manipulative fashion, the essentially hostile fashion that we now take for granted. Conversely, where 'cosmic impiety' continues to prevail, it seems very likely to kill us off in quantity, or at least to make our life increasingly a misery and the world increasingly a mess. Where we continue to fight Nature, in the spirit of the Manichees, humanity will continue to foul its own nest most suicidally, to saw away at the slender ecological branch upon which it perches. We are part of Nature; and as her conquest proceeds, we are more and more obviously on the losing side.

Even so, it is not necessarily realistic to put these prudential considerations first, enlisting theology to help us in a battle for earthly survival. Theoretically and practically as well, a more oblique approach may be necessary.

This is partly because our motivations are complex.

Nominally, most of us desire to live. But this is not an entirely simple desire: something like the 'death-wish' is also a fact. To say the least, the desire for survival is not always the very strongest of our motivations, not the most decisive determinant of our behaviour. It can be overridden quite easily by a variety of other factors—by a zeal for the honour and service of one's gods, as the martyrs of every faith bear witness; by the complex motives that draw men into battle; by a fondness for cigarette-smoke or for the thrills of motor-racing; by mere laziness. In the present case it is opposed by a very strong motivation. Manichaeanism was always a religious outlook, often a religious passion, sometimes a fanaticism; and for many people nowadays, its chief current version—'Man's Conquest of Nature'—provides something like a crusade, a holy war. In the eyes of such people, it is a self-justifying enterprise, a Cause which justifies also any attendant sacrifice, any amount of suffering; and they look with pitying contempt upon those who offer chicken-hearted questionings of the end and the purpose. This spirit often becomes explicit when such enterprises as the supersonic air-liner are under discussion: one becomes aware of a blind dedication, not likely to be deterred by any talk of pointlessness or folly or danger. And even where this kind of fanaticism is weak or absent, it seems unlikely that the fear of environmental disaster will cause us to mend our ways on anything like a sufficient scale and at anything like a sufficient speed. Old habit has enormous momentum, and if it is to be slowed down or deflected, there will be need of some force more powerful than simple fear—especially if, as seems probable, the fears in question are weakened to the last by stubborn scepticism.

The faith and passion of Manichaeanism, if it is to be opposed with any hope of success, must be confronted by an alternative faith and passion, similarly religious in nature but of opposite tendency.

And this will need to be genuine. A change of heart that was assumed or affected for prudential reasons would contain a central falsity: it would not be the real thing, and it could not be expected to bear fruit or to withstand serious opposition. 'The Devil was sick, the Devil a monk would be': the forced or bribed conversion may eventually develop into something genuine, but it starts under difficulties, and can hardly be relied upon for immediate and consistent heroism. It also carries a danger of intellectual impropriety. To an honest man, no opinion, no view of the universe can be recommended by reason of its practical value alone. Self-deception is always possible; but in the full sense of the word, one can only 'believe' something because one takes it to be the truth.

The environmental crisis is a real one, and all pragmatic or prudential considerations need to be taken seriously if they suggest any possible remedy. But if there is any truth in the analysis now offered, in the suggestion that our present crisis is rooted in a modern version of Manichaeanism, this will not be enough. Such considerations will then point beyond themselves, suggesting a higher priority for other considerations, more abstract or theoretical in nature. A Chestertonian paradox will arise: any strictly 'practical' approach to the environmental crisis will turn out to be a thoroughly unpractical thing.

We shall be acting unwisely, therefore, if we embark upon some kind of anti-Manichaean crusade, seeing this primarily as a means towards survival and the good life, as an instrument by which we can master our present difficulties. That old itch for mastery is responsible for half the trouble: it is one of the first things that we shall need to sacrifice.

A shift in motivation is needed: this is a situation of the kind in which one needs to aim off target. He who saves his life shall lose it: the boy who is frightened of being hurt is the one who gets hurt on the football field, and in war, the best way to survive is to think of something other than survival. Our society needs to repent of its world-despising Manichaeanism and its war upon Nature, not in the fear of disaster, but disinterestedly and on the merits of the case—the religious, even the dogmatic merits of the case. This environmental crisis cannot safely be seen as just another practical danger—one that we need to overcome, in our own interests, by a new deployment of our own cleverness, our ability to get the better of things and situations. If we see it in those terms and act accordingly, we shall only be continuing along the old suicidal road. We tend to make this mistake rather easily. In the stress and alarm of these present days, panic-measures are sometimes proposed, such as depend essentially upon some further and fiercer escalation of our war against Nature. Such folly is to be avoided: if we have got into difficulties by kicking Nature around, it is not a sound remedy to kick harder.

More prudently, we should see the environmental crisis as a warning, alerting us to a basic religious fact that we had forgotten, a basic religious duty in which we had been remiss. We need to accept the warning given, but then to forget all about the crisis and the danger, attending chiefly or only to the duty of giving to our environment the much more respectful handling that it actually deserves, and for no reason beyond its actual deserving.

It is as though some husband came to realise, after a stormy scene and a threat of divorce, that he had been treating his poor wife very badly. The scene and the threat will have had their usefulness if, stricken with remorse, he begins to treat her much better thereafter. But if he really gets the message, he will do this for her sake and in mere love. If he only mends his ways because he dislikes trouble and is anxious to avoid the expense and dislocation of a divorce, the outlook for that marriage is poor.

Above all else, we therefore need to attend seriously to the central and abstract question of which this crisis should remind us. Were the Manichees right or wrong? If they were right, hostility to this world is an extremely rational attitude, and our only real hope lies in the escape that death provides; and if we become casualties in the battle against Nature, we shall have died in a thoroughly good cause.

This book is written from the standpoint of one who believes that they were wrong—that Manichaeanism was always, among other things, an error or misapprehension on a point of fact. Any attempt to justify or defend this belief would lead, naturally, into the well-trodden paths of Christian apologetics and into the associated philosophical questions; in particular, it would involve a close study of the problem of evil as it arises in the context of Christianity. One cannot assert the goodness of this world without immediately raising the question of how our experience can be so very mixed. But these larger tasks—necessary though they are at all times, and perhaps especially now— will not be approached here. The thing intended is more limited and specific: an exploratory approach to the idea of an environmental theology. Given the traditional framework of Christian doctrine, given also the suggested link between Manichaeanism and the environmental crisis, what pattern of doctrinal emphasis is called for? and what pattern of morality, of consequent behaviour? If mankind is to recover 'cosmic piety' and learn to treat this world decently once again, what tactics, what disposition of theological forces will best enable the Churches to help that process along?

The full answer to that question will be complex; but at its heart there will lie the simple and obvious principle that an environmental theology must necessarily be, by emphasis, an anti-Manichaean theology. Its prime concern will therefore be to re-connect the idea of God with the ideas of creation and immanence. While having no pantheistic tendency, without compromising God's transcendence and the immense ontological gulf between the Creator and every creature, it will also—and more urgently—stress the other side of that ultimate dialectic, the creative and loving presence of God in all his works, all his possessions, and the consequent holiness of the phenomenal universe.

This theme ought to be stressed endlessly, and at all levels, from the academic to the pastoral and homiletic. It would help, for a start, if the clergy would accuse the modern world less sweepingly of 'materialism': Auden's distinction (mentioned at the beginning of this chapter) should be borne in mind. Technomaniac man is not a materialist, in any Epicurean or hedonistic sense of that word: he sacrifices peace and amenity and life itself to his Cause, he suffers all for the sake of gods unseen. He must be implored to take things more easily, to cease worrying about the control of the universe, which is in other and wiser hands. This world *belongs* to God, not to us: "The earth is the Lord's, and the fullness thereof." In one sense, the whole environmental crisis arises from our habitual but extraordinary assumption that it belongs to us, to the human race, and to this generation in particular. We treat it in a fashion which is not only contemptuous but proprietorial, which is a great folly. By no conceivable title does this world belong to us. We did not make it: we cannot understand or control it except in the most marginal way: individually and collectively, we are catapulted into it by no choice of our own, allowed to occupy it for a short time, and then ejected: the environmental crisis shows up the unreality of any claim that we own it by right of conquest. But perched on this planet's skin, like ants on a football, we swagger and strike attitudes of ownership and mastery. As Shakespeare suggested, it must make the angels weep.

There should be preached to us a more realistic idea of our own standing, a habitual awareness that we live here not as freeholders but as tenants and stewards, responsible always to somebody else, somebody who (if the Manichees are wrong) loves this world and cares furiously about what happens to it.

Such an awareness has, of course, often been recommended by those who have concerned themselves with the environmental crisis and its importance for man's future. "Until men come to believe in their hearts that all life is held in trust from God," says Dr. Montefiore[2], "there can be no valid ethical reason why we should owe a duty to posterity. Once it is believed that men hold their dominion over all nature as stewards and trustees for God, then immediately they are confronted by an inalienable duty towards and concern for their total environment, present and future; and this duty towards environment does not merely include their fellow-men, but all nature and all life." Dr. Dubos speaks in very similar terms[3]: "We must now take to heart the biblical teaching 'The Lord God took the man and put him into the Garden of Eden to dress it and to tend it' . . . This means not only that the earth has been given to us for our enjoyment, but also that it has been entrusted to our care. Technicized societies thus far have exploited the earth: we must reverse this trend and learn to take care of it with love."

But such recommendations, if they are to take effect, need to be well rooted in a theology not only plausible and coherent but actually believed as well. In theory, the 'cosmic piety' that is often thus suggested might be practised by an atheist, without recourse to those religious and even devotional ways of stating the matter: after all, that useful phrase is adapted from Bertrand Russell, not some Pope or theologian. And in fact, this certainly does happen: many an unbelieving scientist of high calibre finds himself mentally coerced, by the nature of his work, into a quasi-religious veneration for the universe, and especially for the part of it that comes under his detailed scrutiny.

But if—in the present crisis—such attitudes have become urgently desirable, they need to be well founded; and in the atheist, in so far as he really continues to be an atheist, they can hardly be more than sentimental fancies. Unless there is in fact an involved and immanent God, unless the Christians are more or less right and the Manichees more or less wrong, our position is not in fact that of a steward or trustee: the world is not in fact "entrusted to our care," and there can be no duty of taking care of it with love. The whole universe is (on that hypothesis) up for grabs, and it will not be consistent to talk about it in the language of ethics.

Consistently or not, the finest scientific minds will perhaps continue to work out their own 'cosmic piety'. But pure science is not what causes the present trouble; and we cannot place that kind of hope in the technological mind, which seems naturally prone to domination rather than to reverence. "It is in the nature of techniques to lead the mind into temptation," says Gabriel Marcel[4]: he is referring to the temptations of power and pride, against which the traditional remedy is 'wisdom'. But wisdom is eroded by aggressive cleverness.

It seems possible, in fact, that our survival may actually depend upon religion; and not merely upon 'religion' in general, but upon a religion which is specifically Christian, at least to the point of being strongly anti-Manichaean. In a new sense, secondary but still genuine, it may turn out that only Christianity can save the world.

But it can only effect this as a kind of by-product, arising from its own authenticity in our own minds and lives, which in turn must depend upon our attending to God and to his creation's goodness more seriously than to any question of our own immediate well-being, or even our own survival. We must seek first the Kingdom.

Tactically speaking, an environmental theology will therefore need to resist and oppose whatever separates the idea of God from the ideas of creation and immanence: very firmly, it will need to contradict and refute every kind of deism, every suggestion of a wholly remote God, not involved in this world. In particular, Christians will need to face the fact that while their religion is not in conflict with evolutionary science[5], it very definitely is in conflict with the evolutionary habit of the modern imagination, the idea that this universe "just growed" like Topsy, or was made by a half-deified 'Evolution' distinct from God. There will be a hard fight at this point: people can be expected to cling, with some passion, to the wholly illusory notion that this Manichaean or dualistic habit of the mind is somehow founded upon scientific knowledge. Here and at certain other points, those who speak up for 'cosmic piety' must expect to suffer unjust accusations of obscurantism. These are unlikely to be put forward, however, by well-informed scientists.

If the goodness of this creation is to be stressed, the problem of our suffering—and of evil in general—will necessarily arise at once; and of all the tasks that an environmental theology will need to undertake, perhaps the greatest is the task of facing this question squarely and of making the Christian response to it a matter of habitual daily consciousness. If Christianity is anything at all, it is an answer to that question: not 'an answer' in some facile sense, but rather a resolution, a dissolution, a collapsing of the problem. As such, it can be put across in this century as in any other; and it needs to be put across with great emphasis, if only because every real alternative is more or less Manichaean in tendency. We have collectively misused a good world: almost inevitably, where this principle is denied or forgotten, people will drift or plunge into the idea that we have been trapped in a bad one.

But the Christian view cannot be put across where there is bashfulness about the terms of the problem, and in particular about the idea of the Fall of Man and Original Sin. Except where pride and self-righteousness are wholly in possession, it ought to be possible to sell this idea on its attraction; it is, as Chesterton observed [6], "the only encouraging view of life . . . It refers evil back to the wrong use of the will, and thus declares that it can eventually be righted by the right use of the will. Every other creed except that one is some form of surrender to fate." But on the Christian side, there is a certain bashfulness about the whole question, with some theologians afflicted by the evolutionary complex, re-stating the Fall therefore in a thoroughly Pickwickian way, in terms of a regrettably slow or unbalanced ascent. Apart from this, there remains that old theological nervousness about the interpretation of Genesis. Neither of these things ought to constitute a serious intellectual difficulty nowadays, but psychological difficulties remain and will need to be exorcised.

In this respect, an environmental theology will need to be boldly unfashionable: it will assert the Fall robustly, on grounds of truth in the first instance, but tactically also, as a defensive measure—against Apollonian Manichaeanism on the one hand, with its angry savaging of the environment, and against Dionysiac Gnosticism on the other, with its repudiation of the actual, its preference for the unbounded ecstasies of inward fantasy.

The people chiefly concerned will not easily be impressed. The Apollonian fathers will condemn such a theology as being restrictive and reactionary: the Dionysiac sons will find it impossibly square and bourgeois. It will certainly involve some radical changes in our habitual attitudes, and in our behaviour as well: the Manichaean bug has got into our culture's bloodstream, and the task of disinfestation will be an arduous one.

But it is a necessary task, and not only because our survival is at stake. In the long run, our temporal survival is a lost cause anyway: there are more serious matters.

Doctrinally speaking, an environmental theology will therefore put first things first. In a fashion highly 'traditional' and somewhat alien to the present-day thinking even of many Christians, it will concentrate initially upon the paradoxical things said and implied at the very beginning of the Bible and in the opening words of either Creed —God's creative presence in his dearly-loved work; the consequent holiness of matter, our own persons included, and the given circumstances of our ordinary life; the Fall, our collective and culpable spoiling of an otherwise happy scene. Only upon that foundation, firmly established and deeply entrenched, will it erect the lofty structure of redemption and sacrament and of the additional and extraordinary goodness thus made available. It will clarify the question before proposing the answer.

And from the start, it will preach 'cosmic piety' as a primary religious duty—perhaps by implication, probably without using that phrase, but resoundingly.

In the field of applied religion, of morals as against doctrine, this will involve the supplementary preaching of two rather unpopular virtues. In the first place, it will urge upon mankind a certain collective humility. This does not mean that it will take a low total-depravity view of human nature, or deny the old doctrine of man's special dignity and vocation, his qualified lordship over this world. Humility does not work like that. The humble man is not the man who has a poor opinion of himself: he is, rather, the man whose merit and standing, whatever it may be, is not the object of his own habitual and anxious attention—the man, therefore, who feels no particular need to assert himself or dominate. At present, in its fretful desire to conquer this planet and outer space as well, our race displays collectively the vulgar assertiveness that we can sometimes observe (but never with much admiration) in the insecure, under-confident, alienated individual. Such collective behaviour is not called for: it is a loutishness. Perhaps, like much individual loutishness, it calls for sympathy and reassurance rather than for rebuke. At the merely natural level, 'cosmic piety' suggests that man is a very exceptional and splendid and sacred thing indeed, a lord of creation certainly and already, while Christianity develops this idea to almost extravagant heights. A sound environmental theology will offer us both reassurance and a degree of pained rebuke, a hint that we might do well to forget the boring obsession with conquest and think of happier things. It will suggest for man, in this life, a more gentle and indeed a more aristocratic role than that of the chip-on-shoulder lout, the swaggering bully, the exploiter, the tyrant: it will beseech him to enact, towards the rest of creation, the high relaxed courtesy that comes naturally to the humble.

In the second place, it will suggest for us a degree of practical asceticism: applied in daily life, it will certainly involve us all in a definitely simplified mode of existence, such as might seem alarmingly austere by the fat standards of today. It will probably be a much happier mode of existence, once we have got used to it; but in the early stages, it will dictate a rather painful mortification of the desire to control and the desire to dominate, and of general self-indulgence too. It will encourage us to be less greedy, less demanding, to have a more positive attitude towards existence as such, towards experience as given: if we still use the expression 'standard of living', this kind of theology will help us to give it a meaning less ridiculous than it has now. Thus sobered, we would shed many of the fretful complexities of present-day life—with reluctance at first, but soon with relief.

This would not be the kind of asceticism that despises and rejects the world: it would have exactly the opposite character, being rooted in an awareness of the enormous good that resides in even a very little—in commonplace things and small quantities and familiar routines. As against the cult of grievance and complaint and exacting demands, it would encourage us to learn something from the old Moslem woman in a poor country who was once heard to say, without irony: "Allah is very good to us; we get something to eat almost every day."

We may react to this prospect with immediate horror: if so, the habit of our mind comes under suspicion at once. Any life, even a short and deprived life, comes to us as pure undeserved gift: rationally speaking, gratitude is the proper first response to it. A kind of incipient Manichaeanism is implied if our first response is restless and assertive and demanding: in effect, we are then denying the inherent goodness of all being, asserting that experience is only tolerable in certain highly specialised and elaborated luxury-versions. You criticise the given universe if you make impatient demands upon it, if you call for modification and particular arrangements: cars and champagne are excellent things, but if you call for them too insistently, you will be denying the more radical goodness of feet and water. And in the same way, while political *activisme* will often be necessary in particular situations, and even the occasional reluctant revolution, we should profoundly distrust the attitude which is commonly verbalized as the desire 'to make a better world'. There is a lot to be said for this one.

Even so, the prospect of any kind of asceticism may well frighten us: we belong to a society which tries to believe—against the consistent testimony of the ages and our own experience too—that happiness can be secured by the widest possible immediate satisfaction of felt desires. And this would be a very human reaction, with much to commend it, if the practical choice lay between such an asceticism on the one hand and an easy life on the other, with all epicurean comforts and pleasant indulgences for all of us. But the choice is not of this kind. Quite apart from the major threat represented by the environmental crisis, twentieth-century living already involves us in increasingly severe kinds of stress and discomfort and shortage and discontent, and in particular in a great loss of liberty.

This is not what we expected. We embarked upon our conquest of Nature, hoping to enjoy—before too long—the wealth and freedom of the conqueror. But aggressive war does not always work out on precisely the lines intended: in the moment of victory, the conqueror is rather likely to find himself enslaved. "As man more and more dominates the earth (with domination seen as one expression of control) he seems to cease to be its master, in another sense of the word control, to a proportionate degree. For if control is taken to mean the ability to have the kind of life one wants when one wants it, then this is precisely what most men cannot have. In his present condition man has only one prospect: to live in an ever more crowded, manipulated environment" [7]. In an acute analysis of another aspect of this problem, C. S. Lewis pointed out that a genuine dictatorship can be involved on the one hand, a genuine slavery on the other. "What we call Man's power over Nature turns out to be a power exercised by some men over other men with Nature as its instrument . . . At the moment, then, of Man's victory over Nature, we find the whole human race subjected to some individual men, and those individuals subjected to that in themselves which is purely 'natural'—to their irrational impulses . . . Man's conquest of Nature turns out, in the moment of its consummation, to be Nature's conquest of Man" [8].

In many senses, we seem to be in real danger of ending up on the losing side; and we may have to choose between the voluntary asceticism of the free man and the forced asceticism of the prisoner. A sound environmental theology will not only train us to make the right decision; it will help us to make that decision in good time, while the possibility of real choice still remains.

Let us hope that we listen to it, preparing ourselves in advance for a situation in which the attractively easy answer to our problems is likely to be the disastrous answer. More and more extensively, this is going to be the grammar of our predicament: those diehards who still cling to the values of an impulse-following society are going to have a bad time over these next few years, and when the crunch comes, they are unlikely to be among the survivors.

Seven

It may well be objected, at this point, that if our future depends upon humanity's early and widespread acceptance of more or less Christian habits of mind and behaviour—and in a specialised version, rather different in emphasis from what the Churches are saying at present—the outlook must be bleak.

The outlook *is* bleak: on any reckoning, it seems that we face serious environmental disaster, and that this can only be avoided or mitigated (if at all) by radical changes in our values and in our consequent behaviour. Each one of us can form his own opinion about how likely this is to happen in fact; and many of us, after studying the picture, will reach a pessimistic conclusion and turn to Stoic fortitude, or perhaps to eat-drink-and-be-merry frivolity, or perhaps to the other-worldly hopes of religion. One or another of these options may quite possibly constitute our best course of action: the more obvious secular hopes are losing much of their long-term plausibility.

No panacea is here proposed, and apart from a miracle of grace, none seems likely to be available. Something will be gained, however, if we become a little more precise about the change of heart that seems to be called for; and to that limited task of clarification, this book is wholly addressed.

It may be as well, even so, to conclude with some consideration of the consequences that follow, in the field of more or less practical action, where the proposed theological view of the matter is accepted. A kind of 'cosmic morality' is indicated and needs some working-out: it will lead us to act and abstain in this way and that, partly because we love and revere the delicate creation and wish it no harm, and partly in order to acquire that desirable state of mind. About each new project, about each proposed development of our civilisation, we shall need to sort out our ideas, asking how far it is consistent with the 'cosmic piety' that we shall have to learn chiefly by practising it.

Conversely, our actual behaviour at any stage will provide us with a useful diagnostic tool. In so far as any activity can be seen as having an essentially impious or Manichaean character, its continued practice—and, above all, its continued acceptance and justification in society—can be taken to indicate an underlying continuance of hostility towards Nature, a failure to learn the lesson of 'cosmic piety', a collective obstinacy in bad religion. It does not in the least follow that such activities ought to be prevented by law: this will sometimes be the right remedy but very often not, and the decisive thing will always be the prevalent values, the prevalent state of faith and charity.

As already suggested, it will be our most practical course of action to put this religious motivation first, worrying much less about a survival that is temporary at the best, and worrying hardly at all about progress and development and conquest and our precious 'standard of living'. The important thing will be the cultivation of an objectively worthy and well-mannered handling of the environment, considered as God's work and property. If we thus seek first the Kingdom, those other things will—up to a point—be added unto us: otherwise, they are likely to prove very elusive indeed. The great lesson taught by the environmental crisis is that they cannot be captured forcibly in the course of a violent war against Nature. Our temporal well-being will be achieved lovingly or not at all.

We thus find an overall perspective, the possibility of a scale of values; and we can use this in connection with the reappraisal of technomania.

Such a reappraisal is already in progress—vaguely, for the most part, and without the benefit of any guiding philosophy. Twentieth-century man has become aware that something has gone wrong with the relationship between himself and the environment, but he cannot define the *malaise*, he cannot see which way to turn or where to draw the line. Hence, he often proposes remedies that only make matters worse.

Sometimes he feels disposed to see all industrialism and even all technology as the enemy. But this seems unrealistic, unless we are to take a total-depravity view of human nature and so find evil in *all* our conative behaviour[1]. In varying kinds and degrees, man was from the start an industrial and technological animal: if we look only at his activities and not at his motivations, we see a continuous progression from the stone axe to the computer, with no point of sharp qualitative change, no point at which some Rubicon was thoughtlessly but disastrously crossed.

But some kind of a line has to be drawn somewhere. It happens occasionally that a few dedicated people opt out of the technological society altogether, and try to establish a little community on simple-life back-to-Nature lines, with compost and homespun. Such experiments seldom endure, partly because an impossible casuistry is generated by the attempt. What concessions are to be made? Artifical fertilisers will probably be excluded, on grounds both mystical and scientific. But what about mechanical cultivators, and electric motors to help the craftsman? And what about factory-made implements, spades and chisels that are possibly tainted by their enemy origin? In acrimonious arguments about such fine points, a brotherhood of this kind will often dissolve.

Such issues are real, even so; and for society at large, there are analogous questions that need to be taken seriously. There is crudity, but some truth as well, in the vague idea that industrialism and technology, as we understand those words today, constitute at least a distressing symptom of the disease. They need reappraisal, if only for political reasons: it seems that we cannot have an advanced industrial society without choosing between the moral squalors of capitalism and the moral squalors of communism. Perhaps we need a simpler, more 'primitive' kind of society, if only to save us from the necessity of making that dismal choice.

Feelings more or less of this kind are certainly widespread, though by no means universal. For a long time now, the public and official side of our society has proceeded—in high Faustian pride—on the assumption that Nature has to be conquered, that it is our chief business to *do* things to the environment, and that all technology is therefore good technology. This faith, applied in practice, has tended to further the influence of the basic Manichaeanism that was its own origin—the mentality which sees this world as an adversary. Belief and action, when they are compatible, tend always to fortify each other.

That faith was never, of course, total: there were always under-currents of suspicion about some kinds of technology, and even about science itself. At one level, the popular imagination could look upon that white-coated figure in the laboratory as a glamorous hero, a pioneer, a maker of the new golden future; but at a level possibly deeper, it could very easily cast him for the role of devil or villain. He knew mysteries and held powers that were beyond other men's comprehension: like an old woman suspected of witchcraft in some village of Shakespeare's time, and for very much the same reason, he was a natural object of distrust. Pulp fiction exploited this theme luridly: the mad or evil scientist provided an element of agreeable terror in much of our childhood reading.

And about industrialism, our feelings have been similarly mixed. We enjoyed the benefits conferred, but we disliked the hell created, in the landscape and in the lives of those who did the work. Presumably that price had to be paid, but we preferred other people to pay it. Many novelists have studied the regional tensions that have arisen, in modern England, from the fact that while the dirt and squalor of industrialism was largely concentrated in the Midlands and the North, the consequent wealth tended to be enjoyed by softer people in the relatively unspoilt South.

With marginal misgivings, however, most of us went along with that scientific and technological complex, that religion of the post-religious age, spectacular in its achievement, Manichaean in its ultimate principle and its ultimate appeal. Only a few eccentrics would criticise it radically and not many of these would actually renounce its concrete benefits. The present writer once attended a conference on the evils of modern technology and the need for a simpler life: he, and almost everybody else present, had arrived at the place of the conference by jet air-liner.

But now there does appear a certain vague change of heart, a weakening in faith. It is not only because he fears environmental disaster that technological man has started to call himself in question. Psychologically and morally too, his characteristic values are beginning to display serious insufficiency or worse.

This can be illustrated in various ways. Consider the serious question of food. 'Factory farming' is (in its way) a most ingenious thing, a skilful adaptation of technological method to biological subject-matter so as to meet a basic human need easily and cheaply. None the less it is coming in for sharp criticism, and not only because we would prefer our veal and our eggs and our chicken-meat to contain no frightening drugs or hormones. Perhaps vaguely but with increasing vehemence, many people are coming to suspect that it may be actually *wrong*—a sin against 'cosmic piety', perhaps—to treat animals in the heartless fashion that seems to be involved by these highly profitable methods of food production.

Similar misgivings are felt in many other connections. The concepts of progress and development, followed out uncritically, seem likely to submerge England in cars and in the concrete that has to be laid down to accommodate the cars. Do we really want this to happen? Any appeal to democratic principle, to public opinion, will yield an equivocal answer: everybody wants to have a car, but nobody wants to have the kind of England that will come when everybody has a car or two. Being thus split-minded, we postpone endlessly our facing of a serious question, leaving the whole matter to the predictable governance of those who make money out of the present situation. But the question is a real one. Do we want, do we need to take some kind of stern decision, so that cars will no longer be allowed to reproduce their kind without limit? Perhaps— as an American writer[2] has suggested, we shall defer our decision "until a thermal inversion, combined with a traffic jam out of Godard's *Weekend*, asphyxiates thousands on a freeway to nowhere."

We can perhaps regard the whole vast transportation complex as one single problem, one single offence—the almost idolatrous tendency by which we sacrifice all things to mere mobility, homes and fields to roads and airports, resources and amenity and (on a huge scale) life itself to the supreme purpose of conveying people and things from one place to another. Here, if anywhere, technology has plainly and cancerously become technomania: a recovered 'cosmic piety' might enable us to sit still and get our breath back and remember what peace and quiet were like, discovering also the human value of neighbourhood living and a neighbourhood economy.

That restlessness, that addiction to mere mobility, suggests a strong collective feeling of alienation and a desire to escape. Happy rooted people, appreciative of the given world, seldom feel it. But it has come to take a high place among the official orthodoxies of our society, which erects movement into something like an absolute value, and thus rushes headlong into much ugliness and stress and absurdity.

No less than the land, the skies are thereby afflicted. Do we really want to have more and more air-liners, more and more airports, indefinitely? At the time of writing, a heated debate is in progress about the particular tract of English countryside that is to be ruined and made hideous so that London can have a third airport. Nobody wants to have the noisy monstrosity as a neighbour, apart from those who expect to make money out of it. The official and orthodox view is that there has to be growth, development, progress, and that one community or another must therefore be chosen to suffer. But now, increasingly but on a still modest scale, the values implied in such a view are being recognised as insufficient and somewhat barbaric. By what criterion can the unlimited multiplication of air travel, with the consequent noise and pollution, be regarded as a contribution to 'progress'? In the classic left-wing understanding of that word, it might be regarded as having the opposite or reactionary character: it constitutes a direct attack on the people's standard of living, undertaken for the profit of one minority and the convenience of another.

The supersonic air-liner is almost the extreme case. By the standards of technomaniac man, this enterprise constitutes 'progress' in that particular field: it is the desirable and indeed the destined next step forward. But by any other standard, it seems pointless. It has not been suggested that anybody needs, or even desires, to travel at that physiologically injurious speed; and it is not clear why the rest of us should be compelled to endure the machine's infernal noise, while at the same time having to pay the phenomenal price of its development. What on earth is it supposed to be *for?*

Beyond this, more and more of us look with dismay upon the supreme vanity and extravagance of the space-flight programme. In a hungry world, this seems to have the character of what old-fashioned Catholics call 'mortal sin': all attempts to justify it stink of the *hubris* that is—in nearly all moral systems—the first and the most doom-laden of sins. In attempting to defend the moon-shot of Christmas, 1968, *Time* said: "Western man is Faust, and if he knows anything at all, he knows how to challenge Nature, how to dare against dangerous odds and even against reason" [3]. Apt words indeed; and if we still value reason sufficiently to learn an obvious lesson, we can remember that *hubris* is classically pursued by Nemesis and that Faust goes to Hell.

More generally, in matters less dramatic, there seems to be some kind of a swing away from the values that technological man has hitherto taken for granted. Do we really want to live in urban apartments or suburban houses, working all day at the factory or the office, and then coming home to processed food and mechanised entertainment? Life has been led in many uglier circumstances: even so, is this our concept of the good life, is this the best that we desire for our children? When a 'high standard of living' is mentioned, can we plausibly and decently understand this to mean 'a high rate of consumption of manufactured goods and supplies'?

Do we *want* to continue on our present course, even if this turns out to be possible?

"The one possible aspect of the future seldom discussed by those who try to imagine the world-to-be," says Dr. René Dubos[4], "is that human beings will become bored with automated kitchens, high-speed travel, and the monitoring of human contacts through electronic gadgets. People of the year 2000 might make nonsense of the predictions now being published in the proceedings of learned academies and in better-life magazines, simply by deciding that they want to regain contact with the natural forces that have shaped man's biological and mental beings."

Tendencies in roughly this direction are already apparent: for one thing, university students in many countries are leaving the sciences and the technologies—steadily and on a large scale—for social studies and the arts. More generally, many of the young are losing interest in the mundane tasks that are needed to keep a technological civilisation going, and also in the values of a consumer-society, the outlook which defines the good life in terms of affluence and possessions. They might see things differently if—like their parents—they had lived through a major depression; and the cults that they pursue as alternatives to technomania and conspicuous consumption are open to various kinds of weighty objection. Even so, this development (which is not confined to the young) is a welcome one. If technomania is to be brought under control and the world used more gently, our needs as well as our methods will have to be reappraised.

This part of the task, the distinguishing of real human needs from fictitious needs, will not be easy. We live under a huge incessant pressure of advertising and salesmanship, and we have come to take this for granted, together with the world of illusion that it obtrudes upon our minds, with greater or less success according to our own intelligence and resistance. We take all this too much for granted. It seldom shocks us, it seldom strikes us as a degrading thing that we depend upon an economy which can only be kept afloat by a continual, massive, and very expensive programme of lying—by the deceptive stimulation of unreal needs, and then by insistent falsehood about the possibility of buying satisfaction.

The objections to this situation are not only moral: social unrest, for one thing, is inflamed beyond necessity by this artificial stimulation of the desire to possess, this association of success and happiness with the purchasing of things. We may find an easier achievement of peace, as well as an easing of the environmental crisis, if by a discipline less painful than we now suppose, we revert to a somewhat simpler way of life—whether from choice, or under the pressure of necessity. "The new asceticism," says Frederick Elder[5], "would involve a resistance to much of modern advertising, not only because of its banality, but because it is realized that any enterprise that continues to support conspicuous consumption hastens the day of ecological reckoning." Such environmental motivations should indeed affect us powerfully; but with that new asceticism once adopted and embraced, we might also realise—with a shock of freedom and delight—that we had been bored to tears for a long time by all that advertising and all that sales-talk, and had no real need or desire for most of the products offered.

If this happened, it would be no novelty, but rather the finding once again of an old sanity, endlessly witnessed and proved and only recently (in a tensed-up and slightly crazy civilisation) lost. In its wiser moments, humanity knows perfectly well that happiness is not always—or even usually—obtained from affluence and the abundance of possessions. We seek these things avidly, but "happily for our blessedness, the joy of possession soon palls" [6]; and in practice, wealth and the desire for wealth bring their own characteristic stress, so that "a high level of correlation has been noted between national levels of anxiety and economic growth rates" [7].

We know all this; and with some part of our minds at least, we envy those who live in simpler societies. "Many investigators assumed that people who have few and relatively primitive possessions are impoverished, long-suffering, and pitiable," says John E. Pfeiffer[8]; "Certainly that assumption does not hold for the Kalahari Bushmen." He continues: "A hunting-gathering society probably provides more free time for all its members than any other type of society yet evolved."

But knowing this, we still crowd masochistically into those rich dirty cities, forfeiting all hope of real leisure and of many other amenities. "All over the world, the most polluted, crowded, and brutal cities are also the ones that have the greatest appeal. Some of the most spectacular increases in population are occurring in areas where living conditions are detestable from all points of view." [9] We behave, in fact, as though there were only a limited sincerity in the desire for happiness which most of us would profess; it is as though we wanted something else more urgently, something perhaps undefinable. A great many writers seem to fight shy of the very idea of happiness, temporal or eternal: in referring to the ideally desirable state of humanity, they use vaguer terms instead, speaking of 'authentic living', of 'becoming truly human', of 'fulfilling one's potential', of 'maturity', of 'the discovery of identity'.

It might be a good thing if, when we are not considering the simply moral questions of good behaviour, we paid more attention to that notion of simple happiness, making that into our chief objective and criterion. There is no great mystery about it: the wise men are fairly unanimous, and experience bears them out. It appertains "to being, not to having, as the moralists in all ages have insisted; and our own age brings no new factor to disprove them. Every wish to experience happiness, to have it at one's beck and call—instead of *being* in a *state* of happiness, as though by grace—must instantly produce an intolerable sense of want" [10].

Even some slight emancipation from the tyranny of possessions would make the reappraisal of technomania an easier task than it now appears.

We can hardly expect to work out a set of clear rules and policies and then apply them simply. The matter is complex, there will be countless borderline cases, and the decisive thing will always be a state of mind and a scale of values. But for a start, we can at least identify a few extreme and egregious cases of 'cosmic impiety'—a few of them have been mentioned in this chapter—and then repudiate them: individually at first, if only by mere disengagement, and then by whatever kind of collective and public action seems appropriate.

Thus, by starting to practice it in ways that may at first be merely negative, we can learn the 'cosmic piety' that we so irreligiously lack.

We do lack it. Technomania is certainly being reappraised, and widely: it is becoming less easy and also less fashionable to believe that all technology is good technology. Even so, the Manichaean elements in our collective outlook are still present and still powerful.

To a degree that may suggest a certain despair, they become manifest in one sensitive and most important field —in our current attitudes to sex, and in our all-but-universal response to what we call 'the population explosion'. Here, more than anywhere else, we make it clear that we lack 'cosmic piety'; that we have little veneration for sexuality and no intention whatever of handling it with restraint.

The sensitivity of this matter is extreme: it is probable that many readers of this book, sympathetic towards the argument so far, will jib violently at its extension to the fields of sex and population.

But if it is valid at all, the argument certainly applies to these matters as well. We can talk lightly of asceticism and restraint and respect for Nature: this is where the shoe is going to pinch.

The Manichaean element in present-day attitudes to sex has already been mentioned [11]; and in an earlier book, the present writer has discussed one of the central issues, the personal morality of contraception, together with the very limited realism and decency of the plans for 'population control' that are so widely advocated today [12]. We are not here concerned with morality in the ordinary and personal sense of the word; and it needs to be admitted that in certain primitive societies, a high degree of 'cosmic piety' has been closely associated with practices that Christian morality would deem extremely lewd. But we may observe, in passing, that men are never 'permissive' about the things that they really value. Where sexual permissiveness prevails today, it indicates a casual and contemptuous attitude towards Venus. In the Christian past, sexuality was hedged around with rules and cautions and restrictions, and some people infer that Christianity itself distrusted and disliked it. While some individuals did have such feelings, the general inference is quite mistaken, as can be shown by an obvious parallel—the fact that among Catholics, the Sacrament of the altar has for many centuries been also hedged around, and in a very similar way, with rules and cautions and restrictions. It would be a mistake to infer that it was considered evil. The point is that it was taken seriously. Sex also was taken seriously in the Christian past, and (with a different kind of seriousness) in societies where Priapism and fertility-worship prevailed. In our time, by a tendency sharply at variance with both cults, it tends to be trivialised. Certain rash theologians rejoice in what they call the 'desacralisation' of sex: it is hardly by coincidence that these writers usually tend in other matters to a clearly Manichaean or Gnostic set of attitudes.

The significant thing, in the present context, is something different from mere permissiveness, in the sense of mere free lechery: it is our society's immediate and almost unanimous response to any threat of overpopulation, within a single family or in the whole world. With hardly a dissenting voice, and quite happily, we at once choose the Gnostic answer of contraception—a technological conquest of sex and of new life, with the armies of abortion and sterilisation in close support.

The 'cosmic impiety' of these practices is extreme: outstandingly, they typify the habit of domination and use, of manipulative superiority over Nature, which—at this time of environmental crisis—we rather desperately need to break. Anthropocentric man, says Frederick Elder[13], "will quickly agree to abortion on demand as an answer to the population question without ever pausing to reflect upon the fact that abortion on demand marks the same kind of narrow-answer approach that has brought humanity to the brink of ecological disaster in the first place." The same is emphatically true of contraception, and the associated refusal to consider restraint as a possible option. In these matters, the habit of 'cosmic impiety' often prevails—and is cherished with deep furious passion—when it has been broken elsewhere: one will often find a plea for ecological and environmental restraint linked—in almost the same breath—with a plea for universal contraception and easy abortion. "Let reverence for life and reverence for the feminine mean also a reverence for other species, and future human lives, most of which are threatened," says an anonymous writer[14] very finely; but on the same page, he pleads for wholesale abortion, vasectomy, sterilisation, and IUDs, and also for the impoverishment of children beyond the two that parents are authorised to produce.

The reverence for life, when learned in this ludicrously selective fashion, is not learned at all.

About these matters, various moralistic things need to be said. But in the context of the wider environmental crisis, it is more to the point to see here a key symptom now, an indication of possible progress in the future. Let us hope that there is some progress: we know already that it will only be achieved at a heavy price, with humility involved, and restraint, and a most reverential handling of this world and of life in particular. But as long as contraception and abortion and sterilisation are widely practised in our society, and (above all) as long as people of honour find it possible to defend and justify such practices in public, it will be frighteningly obvious that we have failed to get the message. Our repentance—in the matter, say, of technomania—will be tactical and superficial: we shall still be Manichees at heart.

As long as this remains true, our prospect is grim. Our race is likely to survive and prosper only in so far as it learns a high degree of habitual respect for Nature, and accepts the fact that this will entail varied restraints upon immediate impulse: within this habit of mind and conduct, respect for Venus and a consequent sexual asceticism will constitute one typical element among many. The kind of mind that finds this an intolerable prospect is exactly the kind of mind that gave us an environmental crisis: the future of a race that thinks on those lines is extremely limited.

The population question remains: to many people—quite obviously—an excuse for Manichaean attitudes towards sex, but a real problem none the less. It is not proposed now either to explain it away or to provide an answer to it. In all probability there is no answer to it, unless a wholesale conversion to 'cosmic piety' leads to a restrained use of sex, within the limits locally suggested by food and space. But while our present habit of mind continues, this is rather obviously not going to happen. Here as elsewhere, a radical change of heart is the only thing that can save us from environmental disaster: here as elsewhere, any proposal to solve the problem forcibly, by technique and mastery and control, will only take us back onto the old suicidal road.

The prospect may well be grim. But at the very least, we can resolve not to discuss this problem except in terms compatible with 'cosmic piety' and a deep respect for sexuality and life; we can refrain from talking about the human race as though it were a *thing*, an object of manipulation and control, with wombs to be turned on and off like taps in accordance with current official policy. If we manage to survive at all, it will be because we have learned to think of ourselves—and of our sexuality, and of all Nature and the whole world—in terms less contemptuous than that.

The central issue, perhaps, lies here—in the question of our assessment of the human condition.

Very often indeed, when these questions of sex and population are discussed, a repressed hatred of human life, and of new human life in particular, comes bubbling up to the surface. And in connection with the environmental crisis, it is often suggested—sometimes in tones of furious distaste—that humanity itself pollutes this planet. Many people see the crisis chiefly or only in those terms, and they call therefore for a sharply reduced birth-rate, to be achieved on a voluntary basis if possible, by compulsion if necessary.

In a sense, they are obviously right. If humanity does pollute the environment, it follows unquestionably that environmental pollution will be reduced—other things being equal—in so far as humanity is prevented from existing.

But here a distinction needs to be drawn, very emphatically. Man, as such, does *not* pollute the environment or dissipate its resources: on the contrary, like every other living creature, he contributes to the cycle and balance of Nature. The environment is polluted and its resources are dissipated, not by man as such, but by certain rash things that twentieth-century man is currently in the habit of doing. And this is not at all the same thing.

None the less, many people talk as though their race were inherently nasty—a pollution in itself, a kind of mildew, defiling the surface of an otherwise excellent planet.

There is, in fact, a good deal of corporate self-loathing going the rounds: proud in one sense, modern man seems to take a curiously contemptuous view of himself as well. His literature is full of the fact: in the most characteristic novels of the day, man is seen as "an ironic biological accident, inadequate, aimless, meaningless, isolated, inherently evil, thwarted, self-corrupting, morally answerable to no one, clasped in the vice of determinisms economic or biological" [15].

If we are to repent of our Manichaeanism, we need to assert and enact not only the goodness of this world but also the ontological goodness of its chief inhabitant, flawed and damaged though he plainly is, tiresome though he can often be to ourselves. Too easily, we forget his continuing splendour, detecting it perhaps in small children or at the time of first love, but forgetting it otherwise. Towards a recovered sense of reverence before humanity, no programme of charity and courtesy and ceremonial would be too much. "Next to the Blessed Sacrament itself, your neighbour is the holiest object presented to your senses. If he is your Christian neighbour he is holy in almost the same way, for in him also Christ *vere latitat*—the glorifier and the glorified, Glory himself, is truly hidden" [16].

We are citizens of no mean city, stewards of a lovely world, members of a race that stands high in destiny, only a little below the angels. Our birth is no kind of a disaster, no alienation of pure spirit into a bad and hostile prison of matter.

A keener sense of these facts would make us much happier. In this book, various courses of action have been suggested that might bring the lesson home to us. The Churches could emphasise God's creation and his presence in it; and to refute the bitter Manichees, they could stress the principle that evil comes only from the misused will, and is quite alien to the nature of being. We can all put this lesson into practice, remembering that this world does not *deserve* to be slapped around and bullied and robbed in our present contemptuous fashion, reconsidering our needs and our aggressive technologies accordingly. And as one crucial element in this new habit of respect and restraint, we could try to refrain from the sexual impiety that now comes so naturally to us.

But against Manichaeanism, the strongest of all remedies is the daily habit of appreciative gratitude. We may not feel this naturally; but intellectually at least, we can recognise it as an appropriate response to the wholly surprising and undeserved gift of existence, and to this rather amazing world, and to all the apples, frogs, bears, cathedrals, fountains, worms, fireworks, icebergs, skyscrapers, flamingoes, snowflakes, bridges, alligators, honeycombs, girls, books, diamonds, ships, flames, hedgehogs, deserts, butterflies, and wine that we find within it. And for the Christian, a list of this kind will only be a preliminary, of relatively small account.

Where this appreciative gratitude is not felt naturally, it should be cultivated, if only by assiduous verbal expression, by self-hypnosis. Even in lesser matters, we know that we owe thanks to our benefactors. Where the sentiment is not felt, there is a loutishness of the soul that may not be culpable; but if we refuse even the words and the outward forms of gratitude, we are guilty of bad manners in the highest degree. The necessity of prayer—and even the rule of its first formulation—might be considered to begin at this point: *gratias agamus*.

Against this radical duty, there prevails in our day a sad cult of grievance and protest. Many people suffer hardship and injustice and misfortune: their complaints are under-

standable and call out to be remedied. Some of us talk, however, as though a mood of querulous dissatisfaction and
discontent were somehow admirable in itself, appropriate
as a general response to life, more romantically fine than
the bourgeois habits of gratitude and content.

We hear too much of this mood nowadays: when ad-
mired and cultivated, it is a babyish thing, a great fo-
menter of unhappiness and contention. It should be kept
for special occasions. "The voice of the special rebels and
prophets recommending discontent, should . . . sound
now and then suddenly, like a trumpet. But the voices of
the saints and sages, recommending contentment, should
sound unceasingly, like the sea" [17]. And they should be
heard to the painful last, not only when the sun shines and
contentment is easy: in Auschwitz, on the cancer-bed, by
the grave-side, that duty of gratitude remains. Chesterton's grandfather once said: "I should thank God for my
creation if I knew I was a lost soul" [18].

If the environmental crisis kills us all, as some well-
informed people fear it may, we shall die by our own collective hand, rejecting life in the finest tradition of old -style
Manichaeanism. But it may not be so serious, it is probably
not too late, and there are signs that the tide is turning here
and there. We have time, in all probability, to learn the
lesson and thus preach and practice a little 'cosmic piety':
and we have certainly both time and cause for gratitude.

It would be good manners, on our part, to make this
a daily habit—to make it the whole of our prayers, if it
comes to that, but at least their starting-point. And then,
on some windy morning, we might open our eyes and for
the first time catch sight of this world, our rare and fragile
home.

Notes and References

Chapter One

1   See the special issues of *Time* (2 February 1970) and *Newsweek* (26 January 1970), and *Time*'s regular dedication of an entire section to 'Environment'.

2   A good reading-list will be found at the back of *The Environmental Handbook:* ed. Garrett de Bell. New York: Ballantine Books, 1970.

3   *The Environmental Handbook*, p. 113.

4   *Reader's Digest*, May 1970, p. 133.

5   *Time*, 2 February 1970, p. 47.

6   *Time*, 4 May 1970, p. 47.

7   *Time*, 2 February 1970, p. 43.

8   Ib., p. 44.

9   Ib., p. 44.

10   Ib., p. 45.

11   *Newsweek*, 26 January 1970, p. 25.

12   Ib., p. 25.

13   *Time*, 2 February 1970, p. 40.

14   *Newsweek*, 26 January 1970, p. 34.

15   Ib., p. 38.

16   This polarization in the American mind is well treated in *The Machine in the Garden*, by Leo Marx. London: O.U.P.

17   *So Human an Animal*, by René Dubos, p. 114. Lyceum Editions (paperback). New York: Charles Scribner's Sons, 1968.

18   *Time*, 4 May 1970, p. 12.

19   *A Runaway World?*, by Edmund Leach, pp. 1–3. (The Reith Lectures, 1967.) London: British Broadcasting Corporation, 1968.

20 *The Phenomenon of Man,* by Teilhard de Chardin, p. 250. London: Collins, 1959.
21 Martin Litton, a director of the Sierra Club: *Time,* 2 February 1970, p. 46.
22 *The Phenomenon of Man,* pp. 274–276.
23 Ib., p. 276.
24 *Environmental Biology,* an article by René Dubos: *BioScience,* Vol. 14, No. 1, 1964, p. 11.
25 *The Environmental Handbook,* p. 8.
26 Ib., p. 8.
27 *The Decline of Wisdom,* by Gabriel Marcel, p. 19. London: The Harvill Press, 1954.
28 *So Human an Animal,* p. 156.
29 *Time,* 2 February 1970, pp. 45–46.
30 *The Environmental Handbook,* p. 15.
31 *So Human an Animal,* p. 13.
32 *The Environmental Handbook,* p. 32.
33 *Taliessin through Logres,* by Charles Williams.
34 *The Decline of Wisdom,* p. 49.
35 *The Environmental Handbook,* p. 19.

Chapter Two

1 *Apology for Wonder,* by Sam Keen, pp. 162–163. New York: Harper and Row.
2 Genesis I.
3 Apoc. IV. 11.
4 See *Reflections on the Psalms,* by C. S. Lewis, Chapter VIII. London: Geoffrey Bles.
5 See Job, especially Chapters XXXVII–XLI.
6 *Great Heresies and Church Councils* (Le Christ Écartelé—Crises et Conciles dans l'Église), by Jean Guitton, p. 43. Translated by F. D. Wieck. London: The Harvill Press, 1965.
7 *De Civitate Dei,* XI, 21–22.
8 *Summa Th.,* I, 99. 44, 45.
9 *Nichomachean Ethics,* 1096a–19.
10 *Timaeus.*
11 *The Gnostic Religion,* by Hans Jonas, p. 241. Boston: Beacon Press, 1967.
12 *The Everlasting Man,* by G. K. Chesterton, p. 282. London: Hodder and Stoughton, n.d.
13 *Texts and Pretexts,* by Aldous Huxley, p. 27. London, Chatto and Windus, 1933.

14   *The Problem of Pain*, by C. S. Lewis, pp. 1–3. London, Geoffrey Bles, 1940.
15   *King Lear*, **IV**.i.
16   *Last Poems*, by A. E. Housman.
17   *Orthodoxy*, by G. K. Chesterton, pp. 22–23. London, John Lane, The Bodley Head, 1909.
18   *The Everlasting Man*, p. 55.
19   *The Observer* (London), 28 September 1969, p. 11.
20   *The Human Zoo*, by Desmond Morris, p. 8. London: Jonathan Cape, 1969.

Chapter Three

1   *The Mediaeval Manichee*, by Sir Steven Runciman, p. 49. Cambridge University Press, 1947.
2   The reader is referred to *The Gnostic Religion* and *The Mediaeval Manichee*, and also to *The Mystic Vision:* Papers from the Eranos Yearbooks, Vol. VI. (London: Routledge and Kegan Paul.) Some aspects of the subject are treated incidentally, but in very witty and readable fashion, in *Enthusiasm*, by R. A. Knox: O.U.P., 1959.
3   *Great Heresies and Church Councils*, p. 20.
4   Ib., p. 53.
5   *Science, Politics, and Gnosticism*, by Eric Voegelin, p. 9. Chicago: Henry Regnery Company, 1968.
6   *Apology for Wonder*, p. 204.
7   *The Gnostic Religion*, p. 142.
8   *Enchiridion Symbolorum*, Denzinger-Schönmetzer, ed. XXXIV, page 588. Herder, 1967.
9   *Great Heresies and Church Councils*, p. 134.
10   Ib., p. 60; *The Mediaeval Manichee*, p. 60.
11   *Contraception*, by John T. Noonan Jr., p. 92. New York and Toronto, The New American Library.
12   Ib., pp. 87, 90.
13   Ib., 362.
14   *Enthusiasm*, p. 102.
15   *The Mediaeval Manichee*, p. 177.
16   This subject is thoroughly (though not altogether reliably) treated in *Passion and Society* (L'Amour et l'Occident) by Denis de Rougemont. Translated by Montgomery Belgion. London, Faber and Faber, 1956.
17   See *The Gnostic Religion, passim.*
18   *The Mediaeval Manichee*, p. 121.
19   *The Thirty-Nine Articles*, art. XIII.

20 *The Mediaeval Manichee*, pp. 179–180.
21 Ib., p. 16.
22 *Great Heresies and Church Councils*, p. 132.

Chapter Four

1 *The Gnostic Religion*, p. 39.
2 *The Screwtape Letters*, by C. S. Lewis, p. 40. London, Geoffrey Bles, 1942.
3 *English Literature in the Sixteenth Century*, by C. S. Lewis, pp. 3–4. Oxford University Press.
4 *The Environmental Handbook*, p. 20.
5 *Apology for Wonder*, p. 112.
6 *The Rock*, by T. S. Eliot.
7 'Gnosticism and Modern Nihilism', by Hans Jonas: *Social Research*, XIX (1952), p. 450. Quoted *Apology for Wonder*, pp. 113–114.
8 *The Responsible Self*, by H. Richard Niebuhr. New York, Harper and Row. Quoted *Apology for Wonder*, p. 205.
9 See the present writer's *Trimming the Ark*, Chapter I. London: Hutchinson. New York: Kenedy.
10 *The Man Who was Orthodox*, ed. A. L. Maycock, p. 155. London, Dennis Dobson, 1963.
11 *Newdigate Poem*, by Hilaire Belloc.
12 A reviewer in *Time*, 19 September 1969, p. 64.
13 *The Gnostic Religion*, pp. 241–250.
14 *Great Heresies and Church Councils*, p. 122. See also pp. 45–46, above, and the present writer's *Honest Love and Human Life*. London, Hutchinson; New York, Coward-McCann.
15 *Passion and Society*, p. 109 and note.

Chapter Five

1 *Letters of Aldous Huxley*, p. 578–579. London, Chatto and Windus.
2 *The Environmental Handbook*, p. 23.
3 *So Human an Animal*, p. 136.
4 *The Question Mark*, by Hugh Montefiore, pp. 12–13. London, Collins, 1969.
5 C.F.D. Moule, quoted *Crisis in Eden*, by Frederick Elder, p. 87. Nashville and New York, Abingdon Press, 1970.
6 See *The Technological Society*, by Jacques Ellul, *passim*. New York: Knopf.
7 *A Runaway World ?*, p. 6

Chapter Six

1   *The Dyer's Hand*, by W. H. Auden, p. 336. London, Faber and Faber, 1963.
2   *The Question Mark*, p. 50.
3   *So Human an Animal*, pp. 7–8.
4   *The Decline of Wisdom*, pp. 10, 12.
5   See the *Letters of C. S. Lewis*, p. 218, for a good brief statement of this principle. London, Geoffrey Bles, 1966.
6   *The Thing*, by G. K. Chesterton, p. 220. London, Sheed and Ward, 1946. See also Chesterton's *Autobiography*, p. 176. London, Hutchinson, 1936.
7   *Crisis in Eden*, pp. 35–36.
8   *The Abolition of Man*, by C. S. Lewis, pp. 40, 47. London, Geoffrey Bles, 1962.

Chapter Seven

1   Such a view seems to be taken by Jacques Ellul in *The Technological Society*.
2   Stanley Greenfield of the Rand Corporation: *Time*, 19 December 1969, p. 25.
3   *Time*, 3 January 1969, p. 17.
4   *So Human an Animal*, p. 20.
5   *Crisis in Eden*, p. 150.
6   *George Macdonald, An Anthology*, edited by C. S. Lewis, p. 107. London, Geoffrey Bles, 1946.
7   *The Question Mark*, p. 36.
8   *The Emergence of Man*, by John E. Pfeiffer, Chapter XVI. New York, Harper and Row.
9   *So Human an Animal*, pp. 145–146.
10 *Passion and Society*, p. 280.
11 (Ref. fn. 14 Chapter Four)
12 *Honest Love and Human Life:* in connection with the idea of population control, see especially pp. 104–110 and 117–129.
13 *Crisis in Eden*, p. 154.
14 *The Environmental Handbook*, p. 324.
15 Edmund Fuller; quoted *Apology for Wonder*, p. 120.
16 *They Asked for a Paper*, by C. S. Lewis, p. 211. London, Geoffrey Bles, 1962.
17 *The Man Who was Orthodox*, p. 126.
18 Chesterton's *Autobiography*, p. 19.